Believe It
to Achieve It

Believe It
to Achieve It

✦ ✦ ✦

Overcome Your Doubts, Let Go of the Past, and Unlock Your Full Potential

✦ ✦ ✦

Brian Tracy and Christina Stein, Ph.D.

A TarcherPerigee Book

tarcherperigee

An imprint of Penguin Random House LLC
375 Hudson Street
New York, New York 10014

Tarcher and Perigee are registered trademarks, and the colophon
is a trademark of Penguin Random House LLC.

Most TarcherPerigee books are available at special quantity discounts for bulk
purchase for sales promotions, premiums, fund-raising, and educational needs.
Special books or book excerpts also can be created to fit specific needs.
For details, write: SpecialMarkets@penguinrandomhouse.com.

Library of Congress Cataloging-in-Publication Data

Names: Tracy, Brian, author. | Stein, Christina Tracy, author.
Title: Believe it to achieve it : overcome your doubts, let go of the past,
and unlock your full potential / Brian Tracy and Christina Stein.
Description: New York : TarcherPerigee, [2017] |
Includes bibliographical references and index. |
Identifiers: LCCN 2017044389 (print) | LCCN 2017048584 (ebook) |
ISBN 9781524704872 (hardcover) | ISBN 9780143131083 (alk. paper)
Subjects: LCSH: Achievement motivation. | Attitude (Psychology) |
Self-realization. | Success.
Classification: LCC BF503 (ebook) | LCC BF503 .T729 2017 (print) |
DDC 158.1—dc23
LC record available at https://lccn.loc.gov/2017044389

Printed in the United States of America
1   3   5   7   9   10   8   6   4   2

Book design by Elke Sigal

FROM BRIAN

This book is affectionately dedicated to Barbara Tracy, my loving wife of thirty-eight years, and the best mother that Christina and I could ever have dreamed of. She has been our guide and inspiration for more years than we can count.

FROM CHRISTINA

I dedicate this book to my wonderfully strong-willed and persistent daughter Julia. Julia, you are an amazing person and I'm so impressed with your strength, determination, and beautiful perception of the world. I feel lucky to be your mom and grateful to be your friend. I know with your passionate insights and creative beliefs you will achieve great things in your life. I can't wait to see what they are.

CONTENTS

Adopt the Achiever Mind-set

Trouble is the common denominator of living.
It is the great equalizer.

—ANN LANDERS

Perhaps the most important questions you ever ask and answer are: Who am I, why am I here, and what do I really want to do with my life?

Your natural state is to be happy, healthy, joyous, and full of excitement at being alive. You should wake up each morning eager to start the day. You should feel wonderful about yourself and your relationships with the people in your life. As a fully functioning, mature adult, you should be doing things every day that move you upward and onward toward the realization of your full potential. You should be grateful for all your blessings, in every area of your life.

If, for any reason, you do not think and feel this way most of the time, it could mean that something is not right in the way you think, feel, or react to life. Your primary goal is to organize your life in such a way that you feel happy, joyous, and fulfilled most of the time—to shed negative or pessimistic thoughts, beliefs, and ideas that are holding you back and adopt an achiever's positive mind-set. This book will teach you how to do that using the strategies that the world's most successful and happiest people use to achieve what they want.

You Are a Masterpiece

Let me tell you a story. In the Accademia Gallery, in Florence, Italy, stands Michelangelo's *David*, perhaps the most beautiful piece of sculpture in the world. People come from everywhere to stare at it in awe. The emotional power of the statue is almost overwhelming when you first enter into its presence.

Where did it come from? Therein lies the story. In about 1501, Michelangelo was commissioned to create a statue for the Cathedral of Florence that would stand out from all other works of art. (It was later placed in the Piazza della Signoria.) He worked on this statue outside in the courtyard of the Opera del Duomo from 1501 to 1504 in complete secrecy.

When this incredible work of art was unveiled at a large public ceremony attended by thousands, a gasp of awe arose from the crowd. They recognized immediately that this was perhaps the most beautiful statue ever created.

Later, Michelangelo was asked how it was that he was able to sculpt something so beautiful. He explained that he was walking to his studio one morning, as he usually did. He happened to glance down a side street to where a huge piece of marble, brought down from the mountains, was lying, overgrown with grass and bushes.

He had walked this street many times in the past, but this time, he stopped and examined the huge block of marble, walking around it several times. Suddenly, he realized that this was exactly the piece of marble that he had been seeking to create the statue that the Medicis wanted. He had it loaded up and brought to the courtyard. There he worked on it for the next four years to create the David.

He said later, "I saw the David in the block of marble at the very beginning. My sole job from then on was to remove everything that was *not* the David, until only perfection was left."

In the same sense, you are like the David imprisoned in the marble. The great goal of your life is to remove all those fears, doubts, insecurities, negative emotions, and false beliefs that hold you back until all that remains is the very best person that you could possibly become.

We are living today in one of the greatest times in all of human history. There are more opportunities and possibilities for you to accomplish more in every area in your life than have ever existed before, and if anything, it is only getting better, year by year.

More wealth has been created in the past twenty-five years than in the history of man on earth, and the total wealth of the world is increasing and compounding at 4 percent per year or more. More people are becoming millionaires and billionaires today, at a faster rate—going from rags to riches in one generation—than at any other time in human history.

People are living longer too. In the year 1900, the average life span was 52 years. By 1935, it had risen to 62 years. Today, the average man can expect to live to 77 years and the average woman to 80 years. And these numbers are increasing every year.

This means that if you take good care of your physical and mental health, you can quite comfortably beat the averages and live to be 85, 90, 95, or even older. Your job is to learn what you need to learn to live a long, happy life, and then apply what you learn, so that you can fully participate in the greatest time for humans that has ever existed.

Avoid a Life of "Quiet Desperation"

Unfortunately, too many people, even in this world of abundance and opportunity, continue to live lives of "quiet desperation."

Instead of being happy, enthusiastic, and optimistic about their lives and the future, many people are still fearful, negative, insecure, worried, angry, and frustrated. They have mental blocks, fears, and frustrations, all rooted in previous experiences, that hold them back from fulfilling their potential and becoming everything they are capable of becoming.

Fortunately, we know more today about the negative emotions and fixed ideas that hold people back from realizing their full potential for success and achievement than we have ever known before. Sometimes, a single idea or insight that leads to you seeing yourself and your life differently can transform you so completely that forever after, you will feel wonderful about your life.

Starting Off with Little

Let me tell you my (Brian's) own story. I came from a poor home with no money and few opportunities. I didn't graduate from high school. I worked at laboring jobs for several years, washing dishes and digging ditches and wells. In my midtwenties, I got into sales, where I eventually succeeded, and then into sales management, where I succeeded even more. By the time I reached the age of thirty, my life was turning around and I was on my way upward and onward.

As my fortunes improved, I one day took a deep breath and bought a used Mercedes-Benz 450SEL, silver-gray with blue leather upholstery—my dream car for many years. I was able to trade in my older car as the down payment and stretched the monthly payments over five years to make it work, but at last I had the car I had always wanted.

When I took it out on the road and stepped on the accelerator, it would start moving faster and faster until I had to slow down to avoid getting a speeding ticket. After I had driven this big, powerful car for a year, I took it in for servicing to a mechanic who specialized in Mercedes-Benz repairs.

THE POWER OF ONE SMALL CHANGE

When I went back to pick up my car, the mechanic, Hans, told me that he had found a problem in the carburetor. A previous mechanic had inserted a key part backward, thereby cutting down the amount of fuel going into the engine. Hans had replaced this part with a new valve and installed it properly. He said, "You will notice the difference."

As it happened, I was already quite happy and content with my car. It seemed to drive very well for me and went as fast as I dared on the open highway. But this time, when I got into the car, started it up, and just barely touched the gas pedal, the car exploded forward as though propelled by a rocket. I had to slam on the brakes to stop from crashing onto the street and into traffic.

From then on, whenever I drove my Mercedes, I had to step on the accelerator very gently. A slight touch would cause that car to blast forward at such a speed that I would have to brake quickly to hold it back. And this improvement in performance was because of one small valve deep in the carburetor.

One Idea Can Hold You Back

The point is that you are like a beautifully engineered Mercedes. But even if your life is moving along in a satisfactory way, you may have, deep within your thinking, a negative memory or block that can be holding you back from accomplishing something extraordinary with your life. When you identify this block and remove it, you will suddenly begin to make more progress in a few weeks or months than you might have made in several years.

Imagine that you bought a brand-new luxury car, beautifully built and engineered with precision in every detail. There was only one problem. Somehow, during the manufacturing process, a part had been installed incorrectly, leading to the brake on one front wheel locking and not turning when you stepped on the gas. Imagine that you got into your brand-new, beautiful, expensive car, turned on the ignition, and stepped on the accelerator. If one front wheel was locked, what would happen? The car would spin around that front wheel. The back wheels would drive it forward but it would just go in circles, without making any progress.

Here is the point. All you need is one unconscious block deep in your mind, a negative emotion or memory from an earlier painful experience, and your life can go around in circles indefinitely. No matter how hard you work on the outside, you will not seem to make the kind of progress—in your finances, your family, your parenting, your career, or your health—that you should be making. The harder you work on the outside, the less progress you will make, and the more dissatisfied you will feel. You will just go around in circles.

Your greatest obstacles to happiness and success are usually contained within your self-limiting beliefs, those negative beliefs that you have about yourself and your potential that are not based on fact, but that you have accepted nonetheless. The key to unlocking your full potential is to challenge these beliefs and replace them with new, life-enhancing beliefs.

The Truth Will Set You Free

In the pages ahead, you will learn how to identify those hidden blocks that hold you back. You will learn how to release vast reserves of energy, enthusiasm, and desire in a direction of your own choosing. You will learn proven ideas and insights that can change your life.

Josh Billings, the nineteenth-century humorist, once said, "It isn't what a man knows that hurts him; it's what he knows that isn't true." Especially about himself (or herself).

Much of the unhappiness and dissatisfaction in your world today, holding you back from greater success, happiness, achievement, and joy, is based on things that you think you know but that are not necessarily true. When you change your self-limiting beliefs, you change your life.

Let's begin.

✦ ✦ ✦

CHAPTER ONE

Why People Get Stuck

Growth means change and change involves risks,
stepping from the known to the unknown.

—GEORGE SHINN

You are a remarkable person with extraordinary potential. Your brain contains one hundred billion cells, each connected to about twenty thousand other cells. This means that the possible thoughts you can think, positive or negative, are greater than the number of molecules in the known universe.

You are capable, right now, of living a wonderful life full of meaning and purpose, having a positive effect on numerous people.

But before you can realize your full potential for personal greatness, you need to understand who you are and how you got to where you are today.

There Is No Instruction Manual for Life, So Create Your Own!

Imagine that you had purchased the most sophisticated computer setup, plus accessories, that you could imagine. You brought it home, took it out of the box, and found to your amazement that there was no instruction manual. You had all this wonderful modern equipment that could perform many complicated tasks, but you did not know how to set it up or use it properly.

You are born very much the same. You come into the world with a marvelous mind, loaded with untapped talents and abilities, with the potential to do extraordinary things with your life. But you have no instruction manual. You have to figure it all out for yourself. And this usually takes years, if not an entire lifetime.

Have you ever wondered how you became the person you are today, with your special combination of thoughts, feelings, ideas, abilities, fears, hopes, ambitions, and aspirations?

The Magic of Changing Your Thinking

Thomas Edison once said, "There are three types of people: There are those who think. There are those who think they think. And then there are those who would rather die than think."

The great majority of people go through life without giving much thought to who they are and how they got to where they are today. As a result, life just happens to them, like a series of random events, with no explanations and few connections between them.

They take the first job that is offered to them, do what they are told, and then other people who offer them other jobs largely determine their career. They marry the person who happens to be standing there when they decide that they don't want to be single anymore. They spend their money on whatever appeals to them and invest in whatever somebody suggests to them. For the average person, life is like a bumper car at the carnival, continually being knocked in different directions, with very little control.

But the fact is that your world is largely created by the thoughts you think, and the things that you do as a result of your thinking. When you improve your thinking, you improve your actions and your results. When you change your thinking, you change your life.

A WORD FROM CHRISTINA

A powerful example of how changing your thinking can change your life comes from an experience with a client of mine. A forty-year-old man came to me because he realized he was tired of not feeling happy with his life. He had a good relationship with his wife and two happy kids, a well-paying job, and a supportive group of family and friends.

He just felt like something was missing and he wasn't able to appreciate his situation. What I realized in working with him was that he had a general attitude of pessimism that was directly linked to his belief that he did not have control of his life. This thinking pattern was causing him to feel anxious and depressed about some unknown impending doom that he could not avoid. We broke his life down into separate parts and identified how and where he in fact was in control of his life.

I gave him exercises to reinforce this new belief. He began practicing making decisions and taking actions that demonstrated that he was in control. Over time he became more relaxed and easygoing. Eventually, his whole attitude changed completely. He became much more optimistic and positive about his life. The turning point for him was when he shifted his perception and chose to interpret things differently. He saw himself as being in control of his choices and decisions, and therefore in control of his future. His life changed completely.

The Mental Laws

There is a series of mental laws and principles that have been discovered and rediscovered throughout history. These laws largely explain who you are and everything that happens to you. As success authority Napoleon Hill wrote, "One of the great secrets in life is never attempt to violate natural laws and win."

THE LAW OF CAUSE AND EFFECT

This is often referred to as the *iron law of the universe*. It was first explained by Aristotle in 350 BC at his academy outside Athens, and was called the "Aristotelian principle of causality."

At a time when everyone believed that the lives of mortals were determined by the gods playing on Mount Olympus and were nothing but a series of random events, Aristotle instead proclaimed that we live in a universe governed by order. He said that everything happens for a reason. Just because we do not know the reason, that does not mean a reason does not exist.

The *law of cause and effect* says that for every effect or result in your life there is a cause or causes. Nothing happens by chance. Even the most random events can be traced back to specific causes or factors.

This law also says that if there is an effect that you desire, such as health, happiness, prosperity, or success, you can achieve that effect by creating the causes that bring them about. The easiest way to succeed greatly is to find someone else who has already achieved what you want to achieve and then do the same things this person did, over and over, until you get the same results.

EXERCISE: Write down the names of three people you admire, whether for the people they are or for something they have accomplished. What is the quality you admire most about each one of them? How can you develop those qualities in yourself?

Here's the first rule of the law of cause and effect: If you do what successful, happy people do, over and over, there is nothing that can stop you from eventually getting the same results that they do.

The second rule is this: If you don't do what successful, happy people do, nothing can help you.

The world is full of people who are doing what unhappy, unsuccessful, frustrated people do, and then they are amazed that they get the same results. But this is not a matter of accident, random chance, or bad luck. It is simply a matter of law.

If you eat healthy foods, exercise regularly, and take good care of your body, you will be fit and trim, and have high levels of energy. And if you don't, you won't. Everyone understands and agrees with this. It is obvious. It is simply a matter of cause and effect.

Your Thought Is Creative

The most important application of the law of cause and effect is this: Thoughts are causes, and conditions are effects.

Your thought is creative. You determine what happens to you by the thoughts you think, especially those thoughts that are charged with emotion, either positive or negative. Your thoughts are like the computer in a guided missile. They lead you unerringly to your target.

Here's a critical point: Once you have initiated the cause, the effect takes place by itself. Once you have pushed the rock down the hill, it rolls by itself, by the law of gravity. Once you have planted a positive or negative seed in your mind, either flowers or weeds will grow. You can control the cause, but the effect happens automatically, whether you want it to or not.

A WORD FROM CHRISTINA

Often, when people first come to see me for therapy, I like to take time to explore a client's "garden" and find out which positive or negative thoughts, ideas, and beliefs have been planted and exist as a part of his or her personal story. Seeds are planted from the time a person is born, by others, and then they continue to be planted by us.

It is vital to identify what thoughts and ideas already exist so that the client can then decide which plants should remain in the garden and which should be removed because they are no longer true for him or her. From then on, the client's mental garden must be nurtured. It contains all the thoughts, ideas, and emotions that make up a person's inner life.

Think About Success

In a twenty-two-year study at the University of Pennsylvania, 350,000 people were interviewed to find out what they thought about most of the time. It turned out that the top 10 percent, the happiest and most successful of this group, thought about two things most of the time: *what they wanted* and *how to get it*. They thought about their goals and the actions they could take to achieve them.

EXERCISE: Decide upon something that you really want. Now imagine that you have already achieved it. Describe what it's like to have attained your goal. How would your life be different if you achieved something that is important to you?

The more that successful people thought about what they wanted and how to get it, the more ideas and insights came to them. These ideas motivated them to take even more actions, which moved them faster and faster toward their goals. When they achieved their goals, they felt happier, more motivated, and eager to set even bigger and more challenging goals. By thinking most of the time about what they wanted and how to get it, they put their lives into an upward spiral of success and achievement. And so can you.

The Foundation Principle

The *foundation principle* of all religions, philosophy, metaphysics, psychology, and success is this: You become what you think about most of the time.

When you think clear, definite thoughts about what you want, backed by the positive emotion of enthusiasm, you direct and channel your energies and your activities toward your goals.

If your mind is a jumble of thoughts, as it is for most people, you will think about what you want on some occasions, and what you don't want on others. You will think about what makes you happy and about what makes you unhappy. You will think about going to work and coming home. You will think about going to bed and getting up. You will think about fun and short-term excitement, watching television, listening to music, and socializing. Because you have no clear, specific goals, your life simply goes around in circles, sometimes for years. You eventually become what you think about, most of the time, for good or ill.

THE LAW OF BELIEF

The *law of belief* says that whatever you believe with emotion becomes your reality. Your beliefs form a screen of prejudices through which you see your world. In other words, you do not see the world the way it is, but the way you are.

William James, the nineteenth-century Harvard University psychologist, said, "Belief creates the actual fact."

You always think and act based on your basic beliefs, either positive or negative. If you have positive, constructive beliefs, you will make good decisions, take correct actions, and get good results. If you have negative, fearful, or angry beliefs, you will take the wrong actions or no actions at all, and get negative results. This is simply a matter of law.

EXERCISE: Get a notebook and keep it with you throughout the day. Become aware of how you perceive situations. When faced with a decision, do you highlight the positives or consider the negatives first? Track these thought patterns and make a conscious effort to view things optimistically. Then track how you feel overall about your day. Make sure you write this down.

All Beliefs Are Learned

Fortunately, all beliefs are learned. Everything that you are convinced of today has been taught to you somehow and by someone. If you have positive, life-affirming beliefs, you will have a happy, healthy life. You will be popular and get along well with other people.

If you have negative, destructive beliefs, you will be doubtful, fearful, suspicious, negative, and in constant conflict with other people in your life.

The starting point of personal transformation is to question your self-limiting beliefs. Any beliefs you have that suggest you are limited in talent, ability, personality, or opportunity are usually not true. They are limitations that you have imposed upon yourself by believing in them. The minute you stop believing that you are limited in any way, your whole life opens up, like a sunrise.

A WORD FROM CHRISTINA

I was recently working with a woman who would experience tremendous anxiety each time she anticipated having a conversation with a particular coworker. She claimed she felt small and intimidated by this coworker and had a hard time speaking up for what she needed or wanted in the presence of this other person.

I had her imagine herself feeling really small, insecure, and intimidated and then I asked her to associate those feelings with an animal. She chose a kitten because they are often shy and timid. I then asked her to think of a time when she felt grounded, confident, and powerful. I asked her to associate those feelings with an animal. She chose a tiger because tigers are powerful and dangerous. I then had her practice imagining herself as a kitten and then a tiger. We did this several times until she felt she could easily connect to the feelings she had associated with each animal.

She began practicing being her tiger self at work and found that the anxiety of talking with her coworker completely went away.

I have conducted this particular exercise with several clients, and every time the client came back to me with a success story. It seems unusual, but taking your self-limiting beliefs and creating a concrete object or animal to represent them allows you to externalize them and become more aware of what mind-set you are operating from. Being able to identify when you are feeling insecure and consciously shift yourself to come from a confident, em-powered place gives you a sense of control and boosts your self-esteem.

EXERCISE: What are three things that you want to do but think you can't do? Why can't you do them? Who tells you that you can't do those things? Who believes you can? Have you ever tried to do these things, or are you just assuming you can't?

THE LAW OF EXPECTATIONS

The *law of expectations* has been discussed frequently over the years. It is used to explain many of the things that happen in society, including virtually every decision made on the stock market and in the economy. It says: Whatever you expect, with confidence, becomes your own self-fulfilling prophecy.

If you expect to be happy and successful, you probably will be. If you expect to be popular and liked by others, you will behave in such a way that makes it come true. If you expect to have a wonderful life, contribute to society, and be respected by your family, friends, and colleagues, that becomes your self-fulfilling prophecy as well.

Perhaps the best attitude you can develop is one of positive expectancy, in which you go through life confidently expecting that everything will work out for the best. And you will seldom be disappointed.

Most unhappy people have an attitude of negative expectancy. They expect to be disappointed. They expect to be cheated or overcharged. They expect to be unpopular or disliked. And their expectations come true as well.

You Can Decide

The good news is that you can manufacture your own expectations, either positive or negative. The choice is yours. The only thing you can control in the whole world is the way you think. If you take control of your thinking, you take complete control of your emotions, your actions, and your destiny.

Your expectations are largely formed by your beliefs. If you believe yourself to be a good person, you will expect to be treated in a positive way. And people will consciously and unconsciously respond to your expectations, whether they know them or not.

THE LAW OF ATTRACTION

This law has been discussed for more than five thousand years. Popular literature suggests that, based on this law, you can have everything you want in life if you visualize and think happy thoughts. Some people think that by the *law of attraction*, whatever you want will inevitably be drawn into your life.

This explanation is partially true. It is true that your mind is a "living magnet." You inevitably attract to your life the people, resources, and experiences that are *emotionalized*, or in harmony with your dominant thoughts.

Emotion is the key to understanding this law. Your emotions, positive or negative, are like an electrical charge that influences your magnetism and attracts you to whatever you are putting out.

The Law of Attraction in Action

What this law means for you is that when you are absolutely clear about something you want, you set up a force field of energy that attracts it to you, and attracts you to it. The essential component for this law to work is belief, or faith. The slightest bit of doubt or negativity regarding what you want will sabotage the process of attracting it into your life.

EXERCISE: Imagine you are going to buy a new car. Decide what car you would like to have and the color. For the next few days observe how often you see that car. You will notice it everywhere.

The Law of Sympathetic Resonance

There is also a sub-law, the *law of sympathetic resonance*. By this law, if you strike a string on a piano on one side of the room and then walk across to a piano on the other side of the room, the same string will be vibrating as the one you struck on the first piano.

In the same way, you will often meet a person with whom you have a sympathetic resonance from the first moment. You have probably experienced this in your own life. Kahlil Gibran wrote in his book *The Prophet*, "In love, there must be an instant communication at the first moment of meeting, or it will never happen."

Many people are attracted to the person who becomes their husband or wife by sympathetic resonance. Their eyes meet across a crowded room and like magnets, they are drawn toward each other. This experience explains why married couples can almost always remember their first moment of meeting.

The Law of Vibration

Another sub-law of the law of attraction is the *law of vibration*, which says that the entire universe is energy in motion, with every substance vibrating at different frequencies. Your thoughts also vibrate, at a level that is so fine that your thought waves can travel through any substance, and over long distances, instantaneously.

Throughout your life, you will have experiences like this: You are talking about a friend who lives on the other side of the country, someone you have not seen for years. In the midst of your conversation, the phone will ring and there will be your friend on the other end of the line. You will say, with surprise, "We were just talking about you!"

This is another example of the law of attraction, based on the laws of sympathetic resonance and vibration.

THE LAW OF REPULSION

The opposite of the law of attraction is the *law of repulsion*. When you think negative, worried thoughts about money, about how little you have and how much everything costs, you create a negative force field of energy that drives money and opportunities out of your life. This is the primary reason why many people remain poor all their lives.

Perhaps the worst thing you can do if you want to be financially successful is to criticize other people who are doing well, people who are earning more than you are. This behavior is usually based on envy and resentment, two of the worst negative emotions. It drives all hope of success out of your life.

But when you admire and look up to successful people, you create that force field of energy that draws successful people to you, which creates opportunities for you to be successful as well.

THE LAW OF CORRESPONDENCE

My favorite law of all is the *law of correspondence*, which says: Your outer world is a mirror-image reflection of your inner world.

You create the *mental equivalent* of what you want to see, experience, or enjoy on the inside and then it materializes, like a reflection, in your life. This is why it says in the Bible, "As within, so without."

Napoleon Hill wrote that in order to become financially independent, you must develop a "prosperity consciousness." Once you have this prosperity consciousness, you will begin to see all kinds of opportunities around you to earn more money. You will meet new people, read relevant books or articles, have doors opened for you, and come up with great ideas that move you toward the prosperity you desire.

Unfortunately, most people have a "poverty consciousness." They worry about money all the time. They worry about how much everything costs, and think it costs too much. They are guarded with their money and suspicious of the intentions of other people. Often because of childhood conditioning, their attitude is, "I can't afford it!"

Good Reflections

By the law of correspondence, your outer world of relationships will be a mirror-image reflection of how you feel about yourself inside. The more you like and respect yourself, the more you will like and respect others. The more you like and respect others, the more they will like you right back and the better your relationships will be in all areas of your life.

Your outer world of health will be a reflection of your inner world of attitudes toward diet, exercise, and personal well-being. If you think of yourself in a fit, thin, healthy way on the inside, you will soon be a fit, thin, healthy person on the outside.

Your outer world of success in your career will be a reflection of your internal preparation and ability to use your knowledge and skill. This will quickly be reflected in your ability to achieve better and faster results, which will move you upward and onward in your career.

Because of these laws, you *do* become what you think about most of the time. Because of these laws, when you change your thinking, you change your life. And there is no other way.

The world is full of unhappy, frustrated people who are

convinced that they can change the outer aspects of their lives while leaving their inner attitudes of mind unchanged. This is simply not possible.

The Discovery of the Self-Concept

Where do your thoughts, feelings, beliefs, expectations, and attitudes come from? The discovery of the *self-concept* in the twentieth century is the single greatest breakthrough in the understanding and unlocking of human potential that has ever been made.

Self-concept psychology says that each child comes into the world with no self-concept at all. The philosopher David Hume called this a "tabula rasa," or a "blank slate." He said that each person begins with no thoughts, feelings, beliefs, or opinions. Everything you "know" to be true about yourself and your world has been taught and learned, both directly and indirectly, from infancy onward.

Of course, each child has a certain type of temperament, which is evident early in life. Each child has latent talents and abilities that can be developed, or that go undeveloped as the child ages into adulthood. But in terms of personality attributes, each child is born with unlimited potential.

The Newborn Child

The child comes into the world completely defenseless and unable to provide for him- or herself in any way. From the moment of birth onward, the child needs an unbroken flow of unconditional love for healthy development, like roses need rain.

The child's worldview, safe or unsafe, is largely shaped by the way the child is treated in the first three to five years of life. When parents give the child a continuous flow of love, approval, touch, warmth, and security, the child develops the belief that he or she lives in a safe world.

BE SPONTANEOUS AND UNINHIBITED

The child is born with only two fears: the fear of *loud noises* and the fear of *falling*. All other fears have to be taught to the child through repetition, usually by her parents, as she is growing up.

Children come into the world with two common characteristics: They are *uninhibited* and *spontaneous*. Because they are unafraid of anything, they laugh, cry, wet or dirty their diapers, throw their arms around, make loud or strange noises, and do whatever they feel like.

Because children are spontaneous, they aren't trapped by worries about what others might think or feel about their actions or decisions. They do or say exactly what they think or feel in the moment, without any concern for whether it is something they "should" or "shouldn't" be doing based on what others believe. They do what is right for them.

This is your natural birthright, to be both spontaneous and uninhibited when it comes to you and your dreams. When you are at your very best, in a safe environment, with people you like and trust, sometimes after a glass or two of wine, you revert to the normal childhood condition of fearlessness, not worrying about anything. You revert to being completely spontaneous, expressing yourself naturally and openly without being overly concerned about what people think or feel, or how they will react.

The Two Major Negative Habit Patterns

Because of mistakes that parents make, especially destructive criticism and physical punishment, children begin to learn *negative habit patterns* early in life. These negative habit patterns then drop into a child's subconscious mind and determine his or her personality throughout life.

In psychology, there are two major negative habit patterns: the *inhibitive* negative habit pattern and the *compulsive* negative habit pattern. We call them the *fear of failure* and the *fear of rejection*. They are the primary obstacles to success and happiness for you, or for anyone.

The first of these, the fear of failure, the inhibitive negative habit pattern, is learned when the child is shouted at or physically punished for trying or getting into new things. Because children are naturally curious, they want to touch, taste, feel, and experience everything in their little worlds. They are completely fearless. They will grab sharp knives, stand on the edges of buildings, and run into traffic. Parents have to spend the first few years of their children's lives stopping them from killing themselves accidentally.

In exasperation, parents say things like "Stop!" and "Don't touch that!" and "Get away from there!"

Even worse, parents will often physically punish children, spanking them in an attempt to discourage them from experimenting and trying new things.

"I CAN'T DO IT"

This soon creates within the child the fear of failure, which is expressed in the thought and feeling of "I can't!" When the child has been destructively criticized or physically punished in early childhood, this fear of failure can then continue into adult life. Every time the adult is faced with a new opportunity to try something new or different, the automatic reaction, usually experienced in the solar plexus, will be, "I can't!"

For the rest of the person's life, the fear of failure will have a major influence in determining what he does, where he goes, the jobs he chooses to work at, the social circle he builds around himself, the way he raises his children and treats his spouse, and almost every other factor in life. The fear of failure hangs over the adult like a black cloud. Many adults react to the possibility of failure exactly like a child who is afraid of getting a spanking for doing something wrong.

Remember the example about the garden? The idea of "I can't" is a weed that needs to be plucked from the garden. That automatic reaction does not mean that the idea is true. It means that it is a thought pattern that has become a habit, and habits can be changed. Through awareness and decisiveness, you can develop new, better ways of thinking and reacting. You can eventually become a completely positive person.

THE FEAR OF REJECTION

The second block to fulfilling your potential is the *compulsive* negative habit pattern, the fear of rejection or criticism. This habit pattern is learned when the child becomes the victim of conditional love.

In an attempt to control and manipulate their children, parents often make their love conditional on the child doing exactly what the parent wants, when the parent wants it, in the way that the parent expects it. The growing child, who is dependent on the love of her parents for her sense of security, soon learns that she is safe only when she does what Mommy and Daddy want. She begins to think, "If I don't do what they want, they won't love me and I won't be safe."

Since the child's need for security is the overwhelming need in the formative years of her life, she soon begins to conform her behavior to the demands of her parents. This is expressed in the thought, "I have to! I have to do what Mommy and Daddy want. I have to do what pleases them. I have to do what they want me to do."

THE PATTERN CONTINUES

When the child grows up, the inhibitive negative habit pattern, the fear of rejection and criticism, triggered by the threatened withdrawal of love or approval, causes her to become hypersensitive to the opinions of others.

In extreme cases, the adult cannot make a decision without being sure that the other people in her life approve completely of the decision. She always has to get approval from someone, or several people, before she can even buy an article of clothing or get a new car. She feels extremely uncomfortable at the very idea of making any kind of a decision in which someone else might disapprove of or criticize her.

A WORD FROM CHRISTINA

The fear of rejection and the desire for a happy relationship with others is a major theme in therapy. I once worked with a young lady in her twenties who was unable to make a decision because she was so afraid it would be the "wrong" decision and that someone would disapprove. The idea of making any choice caused her extreme anxiety. As a result, she found herself struggling in her relationships. She would be so sensitive to the likes and dislikes of the other person that she could never make an independent choice.

The problem was that she was attempting to be what she thought the other person wanted her to be. Inevitably the relationship would fall apart because there was no genuineness or authenticity between the two of them.

Over time, she learned that in order to have an authentic connection with another person, she needed to have an authentic relationship with her true self. Her fear of rejection was deeply programmed into her; she could not accept that she was a genuinely worthwhile and important person. I encouraged her to embrace the idea that she wanted to be with someone who liked her just the way she was, not a false version of her.

She embraced this idea wholeheartedly. She began dating new people and remaining as authentic to her true self as possible. She eventually found herself in a relationship with a great guy who really likes and respects her. They have now been together for more than six months.

She still struggles with asserting her own likes and dislikes, but she is much more comfortable with the idea that if she makes a choice and it doesn't work out, she can just make a different choice next time.

The compulsive negative habit pattern is felt in the form of stress or pain down the back of the body. When a person feels, "I have to!" his or her muscles tense up, starting at the neck and moving down the back.

As an adult, when you feel under pressure to perform, to please someone else, to get a job done on time or your boss will be angry with you, you may start to experience pain all up and down your spine. But when the job is complete, the pain disappears.

Love Deficiency

In some third world countries, children were brought up in areas where there was insufficient calcium in their diet. Because of this calcium deficiency, the bones of their legs never formed correctly, leaving them bowlegged, unable to straighten their lower limbs fully.

A child who has experienced calcium deficiency in infancy can be clearly recognized in adulthood by his or her bowed legs. But a child who has been raised with a *love deficiency* does not show it so obviously on the outside. It is only when you interact with unhappy, frustrated, angry, or dishonest people that you realize there is something wrong.

Virtually all adult problems, and teenage problems as well, can be traced back to the *withholding or withdrawal of love* in the early years of childhood. When you add destructive criticism to the mix, very often you produce an adult who has both of the negative habit patterns, the inhibitive and the compulsive, who goes through life saying, "I can't, but I have to," or "I have to, but I can't!"

Virtually all negative emotions that cause a person to get stuck later in life are planted like seeds by parental criticism or neglect in the early years of life, when the child is highly sensitive, completely defenseless, and unaware of what is going on. Whenever you see a dysfunctional adult, you see the results of a dysfunctional childhood.

Changing Your Self-Concept

Once you are aware of the origin of your negative emotions, how do you go back into your subconscious mind and correct them? This brings us to the role that your self-concept plays in your thinking and feeling.

Your self-concept is made up of the *bundle of beliefs*, primarily from others, that you have taken in about yourself and accepted as true. These beliefs form your reality, whether they are based on fact or not. You will always act on the outside consistent with what you believe about yourself on the inside.

Your self-concept is made up of three parts: Your *self-ideal*, your *self-image*, and your *self-esteem*. Let us examine each of these in order.

YOUR SELF-IDEAL

Your self-ideal is made up of the values, virtues, and qualities that you most admire in yourself and in other people. It is a composite of the person you would most like to be sometime in the future. Your self-ideal is also shaped by your hopes, dreams, plans, goals, and aspirations. The more things you want to be, do, and have in your life, the more powerful an influence your self-ideal will have on your behavior.

Successful, happy people are very clear about their goals and ideals. They take a good deal of time to think about what they most value, stand for, and believe in. They set integrity as the organizing principle of their lives and continually strive to become better, to become more and more of what they are truly capable of becoming.

Unhappy, unsuccessful people have either an unclear self-ideal or no self-ideal at all. They don't stand for or believe in anything in particular. They will compromise their values and principles for the slightest advantage or benefit. They are never happy.

Clarify Your Values

One of the exercises that we do in our seminars is called "values clarification." We help individual participants to decide upon the most important values in their lives and then develop plans to live consistent with those values every hour of every day. Once people are clear about their values and their ideal selves, their whole life begins to change.

A person with very clear ideals engages in specific behaviors (cause and effect), changes his beliefs (his reality), alters his expectations (more positive), and begins to attract into his life more of the people and resources that are in harmony with the ideal of the best person he can be.

YOUR SELF-IMAGE

The second part of your self-concept is your self-image. This is often called your "inner mirror." It's what you look into prior to any event in your life to determine how you should behave.

Happy people have positive self-images. When they visualize and imagine themselves in any part of their work or personal lives, they see themselves as confident, competent, well liked, and effective. In self-image psychology, they say, "The person you see is the person you will be."

All improvement in your life begins with an improvement in your mental pictures, and your mental pictures are completely under your control. You can change your self-image by feeding your mind with positive pictures of the person you would like to be, performing the way you would like to perform.

The work done in self-image psychology by Maxwell Maltz in the 1950s transformed the lives of thousands of people. They learned that when they visualized themselves as the best they could be, their subconscious mind altered their body language, tone of voice, and personality to be consistent with the new mental picture.

When you are mentally healthy, there is always a dynamic tension between the way you see yourself today, your self-image, and your self-ideal, the way you want to be in the future. When you have a clear self-ideal, it becomes easier to continually improve your thoughts, behaviors, and activities so that they are more and more in harmony with the very best person you can be.

YOUR SELF-ESTEEM

The third and most important part of your self-concept is your self-esteem. It is the foundation of your personality. It is the "reactor core" of your emotional power generator. It determines the quality, energy, and strength of your personality.

The best definition of self-esteem is: how much you like yourself. The more you like yourself, the better you will do in every part of your life. The more you like yourself, the more you will like others. The more you like others, the more they will like you right back, and the more they will want to buy from you, be associated with you, be married to you, and have you as their friend.

Throughout your life you will find that people with the highest self-esteem have the most positive personalities, and are the most popular wherever they go. There seems to be a direct correlation among self-esteem, success, and happiness in every area of life.

Fast Reaction Time

Here is the great breakthrough: Just as you become what you think about most of the time, you become what you *say to yourself* most of the time as well. The majority of your emotions are determined by the way you talk to yourself throughout the day.

When you talk to yourself in a strong, positive way, using positive affirmations about the person you would ideally like to be, these commands are accepted by your subconscious mind and immediately influence your thoughts, feelings, and behaviors.

The most powerful words you can use to build your self-esteem are "I like myself!"

Each time you say, "I like myself!" your self-esteem goes up. As your self-esteem goes up, your self-image improves. As your self-image improves, you feel yourself moving more and more toward becoming the ideal person you want to be. Your whole personality comes into balance. You begin to evolve and grow in a positive way.

Take Control of Your Evolution as a Person

Wonderfully enough, no matter what happened to you in early childhood to lower your self-esteem or hurt your self-image, as an adult you can take complete control of the evolution of your own personality. You can make a decision, right now, to become a completely positive person.

You begin today by repeating the magic words "I like myself!" over and over again—ten, twenty, fifty times per day.

Whenever you feel unhappy, worried, or concerned for any reason, you can cancel out the negative emotions by repeating, "I like myself!" until the negative feelings disappear.

No matter what happened to you as a child, you can go back as an adult and reprogram your subconscious feelings about yourself by building your self-esteem higher and higher. The more you like yourself, the better you will do in every area of your life. The more you like yourself, the happier and more confident you become. The more you like yourself, the more optimistic and cheerful you will be. The more you like yourself, the more your life will change for the better.

EXERCISE: Write a list of three qualities you like most about yourself. For example, why are you a good person? What are your best qualities? What makes you a valuable friend, spouse, or parent? Whenever you think about these qualities, you can look at yourself in the mirror and say with conviction, "I like myself!"

✦ ✦ ✦

CHAPTER TWO

What Holds You Back

*The very greatest things—great thoughts, discoveries, inventions—
have usually been nurtured in hardship, often pondered over in
sorrow, and at length established with difficulty.*

—SAMUEL SMILES

Each child comes into the world as pure potential, with the ability to become an extraordinary person, do wonderful things, and enjoy high levels of health, happiness, and prosperity throughout life.

People today can live longer and better than has ever been possible for the human race, and with modern advances in medicine and knowledge, life spans are increasing every year.

As mentioned in the previous chapter, children are born as complete optimists, fearless and uninhibited, excited and curious and eager to touch, taste, smell, and feel everything around them. Have you ever seen a negative baby?

Mistakes Parents Make

Early in life, however, as the result of mistakes that parents make, children soon begin to experience destructive criticism and lack of love. These two behaviors, either alone or together, are the primary sources of unhappiness and dysfunction in adult life.

Destructive criticism is the single biggest enemy of human potential. One could argue that its effects are even worse than those of cancer or heart disease. While those diseases affect the physical body and sometimes can lead to the deterioration and death of the individual, destructive criticism kills the soul of the person early on but leaves the body walking around.

When parents attempt to control their children by giving them love and then taking it away as a form of punishment, they plant the seeds of deep insecurity within their children. This insecurity manifests in a plethora of emotional and mental problems, from feelings of self-doubt, anxiety, worry, and a strong sense of inadequacy and being undeserving of anything good in life, to lack of motivation, fear of not living up to others' expectations, striving for perfection, and inability to confront issues or deal with conflict effectively.

The Two Main Negative Emotions

There are many negative emotions, but almost all of them are rooted in the big two: fear of failure and fear of rejection.

Fear of failure is manifested in adult life as a fear of loss. People who have been destructively criticized as children fear the loss of money, loss of health, loss of position, loss of security, and loss of the love of other people. No matter how much they achieve in their careers, they are haunted by a fear of having it all taken away and having to start over again with nothing.

The fear of rejection is experienced as a fear of criticism that can become so extreme that the individual becomes hypersensitive to the thoughts, words, opinions, and even glances of other people, including strangers. In addition, people feel a fear of disapproval, of not being liked by others whom they are eager to impress.

Fear of rejection leads to a fear of the loss of respect of people whose respect is important to us. People with this fear are afraid of embarrassment or ridicule of any kind, especially in the presence of others. The fear of rejection is the root cause of the fear of public speaking, rated ahead of the fear of death among life's major fears.

A WORD FROM CHRISTINA

I struggle with the fear of public speaking and recently learned an incredibly valuable concept (thanks to my father, Brian). When you are preparing to talk or present to others and the performance anxiety begins to kick in, the key is to assure yourself that your audience, big or small, wants you to succeed, to give a good presentation. They are not there to judge you; they are there to learn, listen, or be entertained.

Imagine You Had No Limitations

We often ask two questions in our seminars to help people see the role that fear plays in their lives and decisions: First, we ask, "Imagine that you were financially independent today, and had all the money that you could ever spend for the rest of your life. What would you do differently? What would you get into, or out of? What would you start doing, or stop doing?"

This question can be a real eye-opener. There are many situations in your life that you would change immediately if you had no fear of poverty at all. If you had all the money that you wanted or needed, you would probably make dramatic changes in your life.

People design their lives to compensate for their fears. They accept lower-level jobs than they are truly capable of in exchange for security. They stay in unhappy relationships rather than risk being alone or unattached. They choose friends who are passive and uncritical so that they can be sure of never being criticized, embarrassed, or rejected.

A WORD FROM CHRISTINA

Fear of not having or being enough is one of the most common obstacles that hold people back from moving forward, especially professionally. I recently attended a professional training workshop. One of the activities was to identify one thing that holds you back from moving forward.

Of this group, 90 percent of the attendees felt that they needed more training, more experience, or more knowledge to be more successful in their field. Prior to the activity, we had each explained our level of professional success. I was impressed with how accomplished each person was. It was surprising to hear that even those with the most impressive résumés doubted themselves.

THE GREAT QUESTION

The second question we ask is, "What one great thing would you dare to dream if you knew you could not fail?"

If you were absolutely *guaranteed* success in anything, large or small, long term or short term, what one big, exciting, challenging goal would you set for yourself?

This question helps people to identify the fears that are holding them back. If you were completely guaranteed success in any one thing that you attempted, you would probably commit to your "heart's desire," the one great, wonderful thing that you were born to do with your life.

The Hierarchy of Needs

Abraham Maslow, the great psychologist, turned the study of psychology upside down in the late 1940s. Instead of doing what everyone else did, which was to study unhappy people and attempt to discern the reasons for their problems, Maslow focused on happy people and the characteristics they shared.

Among other insights, Maslow developed his famous hierarchy of needs. He concluded that each person has a series of five basic needs that must be satisfied, in order, for the individual to realize her full potential.

At the base of the pyramid of his hierarchy of needs is the need for *survival*, the preservation of life, the most powerful drive in human nature. Once a person is assured of her survival, she graduates to the next level of needs, those for *safety and security*. These needs are satisfied when the individual has enough food, clothing, shelter and money so that none of these needs are pressing.

Once the individual has satisfied her needs for survival and safety and security, she progresses to the third level of the hierarchy, the satisfaction of *belongingness* needs. Each person has a deep desire to be a part of a group of people, to be recognized and accepted by them. This is as much a need for an individual as the need for food, drink, and shelter.

DEPENDING ON OTHERS

Realizing your need for human contact and belonging is important in understanding how to move forward when you feel stuck. As babies we are completely vulnerable and depend on our primary caregiver for physical survival and emotional comfort. As we become adults, we transfer our attachments to our peers or significant others, and we depend on those relationships for our emotional health and even our survival.

The reason fear of rejection is so powerful is that the idea of being completely alone feels emotionally life threatening. We depend so deeply on the acceptance and support of others that we learn to suppress our true needs to keep our friends and associates around.

A WORD FROM CHRISTINA

I worked with a young man who had learned that in order to keep his parents happy and attentive to him, he had to suppress his own needs and maintain a cooperative, easygoing manner. He had discovered that when he had strong emotions, positive or negative, his parents did not respond well to him. They began to withdraw from him. He soon learned to suppress his feelings and reactions so as not to lose the approval of his parents.

When he grew up, he became so disconnected from his true feelings that he experienced low self-esteem and self-confidence both personally and professionally. It took him a long time to learn that his personal wants and needs were just as valid as those of anyone else, including his parents.

DEFICIENCY NEEDS VERSUS BEING NEEDS

These first three types of needs (survival, safety and security, and belongingness) are defined as "deficiency needs." In their absence, the individual becomes preoccupied with satisfying them, to the exclusion of everything else. But once these needs are satisfied, the individual moves upward toward the satisfaction of higher-order needs, or "being needs," the fourth of which is for *self-esteem.*

Almost everything that we do in life today is either to achieve feelings of self-esteem or to compensate for its lack. Your self-esteem, how much you like yourself, lies at the core of your personality and largely determines the quality of your emotional life.

In Maslow's hierarchy, once self-esteem needs are satisfied, the individual moves to the highest level, the satisfaction of *self-actualization* needs. Self-actualization, as defined by Abraham Maslow, is "to become everything that one is capable of becoming."

HIGHER NEEDS

Later, Maslow concluded that there are two even higher needs, which emerge naturally once a person has satisfied the needs for survival, safety, belongingness, self-esteem, and self-actualization. These are the needs for *truth* and *beauty*.

Throughout the history of human civilization, you see examples in which wealthy individuals and societies invested enormous amounts of money and labor in philosophy, literature, poetry, and the search for truth. They then invested substantially in art, architecture, jewelry, public buildings, and beautiful homes and castles, all in the search for beauty.

The Fully Functioning Person

The psychiatrist William Glasser defined a person who has achieved the higher levels of mental and emotional development as a *fully functioning person* (FFP). This is a person who enjoys high levels of self-esteem and personal contentment, and who is completely relaxed with himself and the world. The most identifiable characteristic of a fully functioning person seems to be that he is completely "non-defensive."

The FFP does not feel that he has to justify or explain himself to anyone for anything. He lives his life completely in accordance with his own thoughts, feelings, values, and ideals. He is warm, gracious, happy, and charming and is called a "fully mature, fully integrated personality." To reach this level is one of our most important goals.

WHAT HOLDS US BACK

The question is: What keeps people at the lower levels of need satisfaction, or dissatisfaction? What causes people to be preoccupied with survival, safety and security, and belongingness needs? The answer is *negative emotions*.

Because of destructive criticism and lack of love, children begin to develop negative emotions at an early age. As they become adults, these emotions can become more and more intense, and generate additional negative emotions of various kinds.

The main negative emotions that people experience are those of fear, doubt, worry, envy, jealousy, resentment, undeservingness, and feelings of inadequacy, especially in comparison to others.

Fear, doubt, and worry arise when the child is continually criticized whenever she makes a mistake of any kind. Even if she accomplishes something worthwhile, it is never enough to satisfy her parents. In addition, the parents seldom express love or approval, or if they do, they immediately withdraw it if they feel that the child is failing to please them in some way.

BECOMING A FULLY FUNCTIONING PERSON

Your goal is to become a fully functioning person, but most of us are not there yet. As a result, most people look to others to validate the decisions they make. Often when someone else has a different opinion, or makes decisions contrary to their own, indecisive people can feel insecure or threatened. They ask, "Which choice is best?"

A WORD FROM CHRISTINA

Jon is a middle-aged man who struggles to be decisive and proactive in his life. He has a very close family and is one of three children. His relationships with his family are important to him. He often seeks the opinion of his mother and brother. After working with Jon for several months I realized that every time he sought advice from his mother, his anxiety levels would increase. If he agreed with her and did what she said, then she would be supportive and loving. However, if he did or even wanted to do something she didn't approve of, she would stop talking to him for a couple of weeks.

He felt paralyzed, unable to move forward in his life because he knew it meant upsetting his mother and feeling rejected by his family. I have worked with many clients who have the same experience. What holds them back and keeps them stuck is the fear that if they did something new or different, they could lose the love or approval of an important person in their lives. As a result, they can remain stuck in the same place for years.

Envy and Resentment

Envy and resentment are negative emotions that arise from deep feelings of inadequacy and inferiority. They seem to go together, arm in arm, like twins.

Envy is one of the worst of the negative emotions. It is the only one of the "seven deadly sins" for which there is *no payoff* for the envious person. He or she can envy another person to the point of being furious inside, but it has no effect on the target and it gives no benefit or pleasure to the person obsessed with the envy. Envy is usually learned from one or both parents as the result of being continually told that people who are more successful or happy are fundamentally bad or dishonest.

In our society today, the emotion of envy drives most social and political policy, both nationally and internationally. Envy is always outwardly directed, at someone—"the enemy"—who is doing better than the person experiencing the feeling of envy. Because this person is considered bad, he or she must be brought down or punished in some way.

The unfortunate thing about envy is that it can never be satisfied. If anything, it grows and becomes worse over time. And it causes far more damage to the person experiencing the emotion than to the person or group at whom it is aimed.

ADMIRATION IS POSITIVE

Admiring something that another person has attained or accomplished is not the same as envy. It is important to want things that other people have because it motivates you to accomplish the same.

Because of the mental laws of attraction and repulsion, the worst thing you can do to yourself is to envy or resent others. When you do, you set up a force field of negative energy that drives out and repels success and happiness from your own life. The misunderstanding of this basic concept is a major reason for frustration, discontent, and underachievement for many people.

RESENTMENT REQUIRES AN ENEMY

The twin sister of envy is resentment. Like envy, resentment arises when someone feels that another person has achieved or is enjoying a better life situation than one's own. Certain political philosophies absolutely require an enemy, someone at whom envy and resentment can be directed in order to justify the political policies or platform of the party leaders. Don't allow yourself to be trapped into the emotional quicksand of resentment because of what others say.

Jealousy and Low Self-Esteem

The negative emotion of jealousy comes from low self-esteem, a feeling of unworthiness and inadequacy, the idea that one could never really be loved by someone else.

A little jealousy may be normal and natural, especially while growing up and comparing ourselves to those who seem to be more attractive or doing better than we are, but too much jealousy becomes what Shakespeare called the "green-eyed monster." It can be terribly destructive to the person experiencing the jealousy, leading to unreasonable behavior and ruined relationships.

All emotions, especially those that are negative, distort evaluations. A person in the grip of a negative emotion is incapable of thinking clearly or rationally. The more intense the negative emotion, the more the sufferer becomes detached from reality and is incapable of reasoning clearly. He or she then talks and acts in a way that is often unexplainable and completely destructive.

We All Have Our "Crazy Times"

In 1982, a New York writer, Abigail Trafford, who had been through a particularly bitter two-year divorce, wrote a book called *Crazy Time*. In this book, she explained how the emotionally chaotic two years of her divorce caused her to behave in ways that she could barely recognize when the divorce was over and she had returned to normal. She felt that she had been "insane" for the entire time because of the intensity of the negativity she was feeling. Emotions distort evaluations.

Big life changes such as a new job, moving, the birth of a child, and the end of a relationship can all result in short periods of feeling overwhelmed and irrational. Remember Maslow's hierarchy: Humans need to feel safe and secure or they become consumed with satisfying that need. When we feel insecure for any reason, all we can think of is regaining our security wherever it is lacking, similar to thinking constantly about food when we are hungry.

A WORD FROM CHRISTINA

When I am working with clients who are going through a transition of some kind, we talk about the idea that they will probably feel anxious and insecure until they have gone through the change and found themselves grounded again.

Having a baby is a good example. I remember how after the birth of each child (I have three) life seems chaotic and overwhelming. This is quite normal and natural; it's almost always a stressful and emotional time for the family. Eventually, however, everything smooths out and returns to normal.

Five Factors That Create Negative Emotions

There are five major factors that cause people to create negative emotions and hold on to them. To free yourself from negative emotions, you must recognize where they come from so that you can get rid of them, or even stop them from developing in the first place.

1. JUSTIFICATION

The first cause of negative emotions is *justification*. Negative emotions cannot exist unless you can explain to yourself and others why you are entitled to feel how you do about this person or situation. When you are discussing the negative situation, you become preoccupied with justifying your negativity on a variety of grounds. Often you drive along talking to yourself, making your case and arguing vehemently with people who are not there.

The more you justify yourself and convince yourself that the other person is wrong and evil, that you are pure and innocent, and that you are therefore entitled to feel the way you do, the angrier and more upset you become.

2. IDENTIFICATION

The second requirement for negative emotions to exist is *identification*. This means that you take things personally. You see what has happened as a personal attack and feel that you have been taken advantage of in some way.

Another term for this is what behavioral scientists call the *fundamental attribution error*. This means that when someone else does something that hurts or offends us. We blame his or her behavior on some character deficiency. If, however, we do something to offend or inconvenience another person, we excuse it away as an accident, or blame it on outside forces.

If you cannot personally identify with a negative person or situation, it is difficult to generate any emotion, positive or negative, about that person. For example, if you read in the paper that a thousand people—men, women, and children—had been washed away and tragically drowned in a flood in northern China, you might feel a little sadness, but then you would flip the page to the next subject with no emotion at all. Because you do not know any of the people affected, or even know about that part of the world, you do not identify with the tragedy. As a result, you experience no negative emotions when you learn about it.

3. HYPERSENSITIVITY

The third cause of negative emotions is *hypersensitivity* to the thoughts, opinions, or attitudes of others toward you. When a person has been raised with destructive criticism and lack of love, he can develop deep feelings of inferiority and inadequacy. These feelings will manifest as an over-concern about the actions, reactions, and treatment that he experiences from other people.

One positive word or comment of approval from another can cause him to be elated. One negative glance or comment can make him feel unhappy. Truly hypersensitive people often see slights and disapproval where none exist. They tend to imagine that other people are thinking and talking about them behind their backs. In extreme cases, hypersensitive people become paralyzed in that they cannot make a decision without getting the approval of other people, and often lots of people.

4. THE CURSE OF JUDGMENTALISM

The fourth reason for negative emotions is *judgmentalism*, the tendency of people to judge others in a negative way. When you judge others unfavorably, you invariably find them guilty of something. This guilt becomes the justification for your anger and resentment toward them.

In the Bible it says, "Judge not that ye be not judged." What this means is that when you judge others, you actually bring negativity and unhappiness upon yourself. When you judge, you are setting yourself up as someone who thinks he is superior to the other person, making him or her inferior to you.

If you do not pass judgment on another, for any reason, you cannot be angry with that person. It is only when you can make a good case that the other person has done or said something that has hurt you (or that person has failed to do something) that you can be angry.

The starting point of eliminating judgmentalism from your life is to resolve, from now on, not to judge anyone else for anything, unless it is to admire and praise them.

EXERCISE: Most often we judge another person for something because it is something we don't like in ourselves, or we are jealous of her and want to be able to achieve or behave the way she does. The next time you find yourself passing judgment, explore the motivation. Do you dislike a similar trait in yourself? Or do you wish you could behave or achieve the way this person does?

Practice Detachment

The opposite of judging and condemning is the practice of *detachment*. Stand back from the person, remain unemotional, and rise above the situation.

When you judge another, you become emotional, and emotions distort evaluations. The more you judge and condemn, the angrier and more out of control you become.

If you have been brought up in a family with someone who was continually complaining about or criticizing others, you may have developed the false idea that judging and condemning others is a normal and natural thing to do. The very idea of remaining neutral and detached when someone does or says something that you don't agree with may seem strange to you at first.

Another way to stay neutral is to be curious instead. It is not possible to ask questions and become angry or judgmental at the same time. Everyone you meet has a story of some kind; sometimes you can be judgmental because you don't know the reasons for people's behavior. Ask questions—not to support your position, but to better understand where they are coming from.

You will often find that the truth of the situation is completely different from what it first appeared to be.

Use Your Mind Properly

You have a wonderful mind. But it is a double-edged sword. You can use it to make you happy, or you can use it to make you angry. Your goal should be to use your intelligence to keep yourself calm, in control, and at peace, no matter what is happening around you or to you. Krishnamurti, the Indian sage, said, "My secret of success is simple; I just don't care very much about anything."

When people behave poorly, refrain from judging. When people do or say things that seem to be negative and unnecessary, remain calm and detached. Stand back mentally and observe them impartially, without becoming upset or involved.

The best way to stop judging is to *have compassion for* the other person. It is almost impossible to have compassion toward another person for his behavior and judge him negatively at the same time. Even better, you can *bless, forgive, and let go.* Rise above it. Refuse to allow the behavior of the other person to affect you in any way. Switch your focus to something that makes you happy. In this way, you neutralize the negative thought and any tendency to judge another person.

Be Patient and Empathetic

When you deal with a difficult person, treat him exactly as if he was a tired, hungry, irritable child becoming angry or even throwing a tantrum. You don't get angry with a child; you have compassion. You just accept that this is the way children behave at certain times, under certain circumstances.

Another way to refrain from judging is to remind yourself that if you were in the same situation, you might act the same. You can say, "There, but for the grace of God, go I." You may also just acknowledge that all people are entitled to think and feel their own way. Allow others to express themselves the same way that you would want to be allowed to express yourself.

The Sedona Method

There is a method of regaining emotional control in your life called the Sedona method, created by Lester Levenson, in which you are asked to identify the people in your past with whom you are still angry. You also identify the situations from your past that you are still upset about, those things you did or didn't do.

They then ask you two questions: First, "Do you want to be free of the negativity associated with this unhappy memory?" If your answer is yes, then the second question is, "Are you willing to let it go completely?"

It is amazing how many people are unwilling to let go of a negative event that happened to them in the past. They feel that they have earned the pain and paid for it with time, money, and personal suffering. They feel entitled to their pain. In their heart of hearts, they are not willing to let it go. But without the willingness to do so, these people cannot be helped.

TAKE THE PENCIL TEST

Here is the example used in the Sedona method. Take a pencil in your hand. Squeeze it tightly. Squeeze it even more tightly—as hard as you can.

Imagine holding on tightly to this pencil for an hour, a day, a month, or even years. What would happen to your hand and arm? They would become atrophied and even immovable, paralyzed.

What would happen if you clung tightly, bitterly to a negative experience for months and years? Part of your personality would be damaged with anger and bitterness.

Now extend your arm and open your hand with the palm facing toward the floor while you are squeezing this pencil. Here's the question: What is holding this pencil in your hand?

The answer is obvious. You are holding this pencil and squeezing it so hard.

The next question is also obvious: How do you get rid of this pencil? How do you get it out of your hand? The answer is simple. You open your hand and let it fall. *You let go.*

This is a wonderful illustration of the simplicity of dropping a negative event out of your life permanently. With the pencil, you open your hand and let it go. With a negative experience that still makes you unhappy, you open your heart and let it go.

You Decide Your Own Emotions

Remember, no one *makes* you feel anything. No one makes you mad. Nothing that has happened to you has any control over you. No previous event, circumstance, or person can affect your emotions without your permission. It is only *you* who makes you feel anything, positive or negative, by the way that you interpret that past event to yourself.

One of the most beautiful of all emotions is *compassion*. Feeling compassion toward someone means understanding the emotions that the other person is feeling, and then being accepting of those emotions.

When you use your wonderful mind to find reasons for not judging, for letting the other person off the hook, and for letting go of any past hurt, you take complete control of your thinking and your emotions. Instead of finding reasons why the other person is guilty and should be condemned and punished, you find reasons to find her not guilty and let her go free.

Write It Down and Let It Go!

Here is a simple exercise that works for many people. Take a piece of paper and write down the names of the people whom you are still angry about. Write down the things they did that caused you to feel justified in your anger and condemnation.

Then take this piece of paper, rip it up, and throw it in the trash.

In this way, you can use your power of choice to let go of the hurt and pain of the past, to put it behind you or destroy it completely so that you can enjoy the freedom and joy of the future.

5. RATIONALIZATION

The fifth cause of negative emotions is *rationalization*. This occurs when you use your rational mind to put a socially acceptable explanation on your own otherwise unacceptable act. You explain it away.

Because of low self-esteem and weak egos, most people cannot admit that they have done or said anything that was not thoroughly reasonable and justified on their part. Even the worst criminals feel that they are innocent and merely victims of someone, something, or society. They rationalize their behaviors.

Eliminate the Expression of Negative Emotions

Peter Ouspensky, in his book *In Search of the Miraculous*, explained that almost all unhappiness comes from expressing negative emotions. It is the constant talking about and rehashing of a negative situation that keeps the negative emotions alive and growing.

In this sense, your negative emotions can be compared to a brush fire that begins with a spark but can quickly spread out of control. But if a spark lands on dry brush and you put it out immediately, no fire starts or spreads. In the same way, if you stop the negative emotion the moment it is triggered, it quickly goes out, like a small fire, and causes no damage.

However, if you continually talk about the cause of the negative emotion, both to yourself and to others, it can soon grow out of control, like a brush fire, and completely overwhelm your thoughts and emotions, to the exclusion of any other thoughts or feelings. You soon lose your ability to think clearly.

The Worst Emotion of All

All negative emotions, sooner or later, come down to one: anger. Anger is the ultimate negative emotion. All fear, doubt, jealousy, envy, and resentment eventually turn into anger of some kind. This anger is then *inwardly* directed, making yourself physically and emotionally sick, or *outwardly* directed, undermining and destroying your relationships with other people.

All unhappy people are angry. Depression is inwardly directed anger, caused by the inability of the person to express his or her feelings or do something about a situation openly and honestly. The attempt to discover this internal conflict is the foundation of modern psychology, going back all the way to Sigmund Freud.

The primary goal of psychological counseling of any kind is to help the individual "get it off his chest" and let out the negative emotions and experiences that are holding him back.

The primary reason for anger is that the individual feels aggressed upon, attacked, hurt, or taken advantage of by another person or persons. Anger is defensiveness rooted in sadness, a wanting to strike back at someone who has hurt you.

THE EXPRESSION OF ANGER

One of the worst parts of anger is that the more you express it, the angrier you become. The more you talk about, justify, and rationalize why you are entitled to be angry, the bigger the anger grows, like a brush fire. Many people have been angry for so long that they reach the point where the smallest event triggers an explosion of anger. They go through life angry most of the time. Soon, they come to believe that a sense of anger and being taken advantage of is a normal way to think and feel.

The core of anger is blame. The ability to blame someone for something that he or she has done or not done is the essential requirement for the feeling and expression of anger, and negative emotions of all kinds.

It is not possible to hold a negative emotion for any period of time unless you can blame someone or something for the situation you are angry about. The moment you stop blaming, the negative emotion or emotions stop completely, like turning off a light switch.

Accept Responsibility Rather Than Blaming Others

The antidote to negative emotions, blaming, and anger is so simple and effective that it is almost overwhelming. People who have been negative, angry, and unhappy for years can short-circuit their negative emotions almost instantly with one simple but powerful technique.

Since all negative emotion is rooted in blame and anger, which means that someone else has done or not done something to make you angry or unhappy, the answer is simple: Instead of blaming, accept responsibility for the situation.

When you accept complete responsibility for the situation, for whatever has happened, your negative emotions stop, like slamming on the brakes. It is impossible to accept responsibility for a situation and to simultaneously be angry or unhappy about that situation. The acceptance of responsibility cancels out all the negativity associated with the situation or person.

"I AM RESPONSIBLE!"

How do you accept responsibility? Simple: Say the words "I am responsible!"

Whenever you are angry or unhappy for any reason, immediately repeat to yourself, over and over, "I am responsible!" until the negative feeling goes away.

This is an astonishing discovery that totally transforms the life of every person who practices it. Your mind can hold only one thought at a time, positive or negative. It can hold the positive emotion of personal responsibility or it can hold a negative emotion of any kind.

And the choice is always up to you. The only thing in the universe that you can control is the content of your conscious mind. If you choose to hold the thought "I am responsible," rather than the negative thought that makes you unhappy, you become positive, optimistic, and calm, sometimes in just a few seconds.

REFUSE TO EXPRESS NEGATIVE FEELINGS

As mentioned earlier, unhappiness comes from the expression of negative emotions, either internally, externally, or both. If you do not express your negative emotions, they quickly die away.

From this moment onward, instead of using your incredible intelligence to think of reasons why you should be fearful, doubtful, envious, jealous, resentful, and angry because of things that have happened or not happened, use your mind to find reasons not to express your negative feelings, justifications, and rationalizations.

Again, the most powerful all-purpose way to stop the expression of negative emotions is to repeat, "I am responsible!" every time an event occurs that would normally trigger a negative reaction from you.

JUSTIFYING AND RATIONALIZING

At this point, many people say, "Wait a minute! There is no way that I can accept responsibility for the terrible thing this other person did to hurt me. Accepting responsibility would not be honest because I am not responsible in any way."

This approach may be true. You may have been robbed, cheated, lied to, swindled, betrayed, or hurt in a thousand ways by someone else. You may have come back to the parking lot and found that someone had driven into the side of your car and then driven away. In a case like this, you're not legally at fault and you are not to blame.

However, here's the answer: You are responsible for your *responses*. You may not be responsible for what happened, but you are responsible for the way you behave afterward. And your responses are completely under your control. They are a matter of personal choice. Nothing makes you angry or unhappy. You make yourself angry or unhappy by the way that you choose to react to the unhappy experience.

USE YOUR WILLPOWER

In Rudyard Kipling's poem "If—," he says, "If you can keep your head when all about you are losing theirs and blaming it on you . . . you'll be a Man, my son!"

The mark of superior people is that they can exert their willpower and self-discipline to keep themselves calm, aware, and effective, no matter what is going on around them. All great men and women have developed the ability to remain "cool under fire."

But remember, emotions distort evaluations. The minute you begin to blame someone else and become angry for what has occurred, you begin to lose your ability to think clearly and decide intelligently. You become a slave to your emotions. You can very quickly become swept away and find yourself doing and saying things that you later regret.

FIND REASONS *NOT* TO EXPRESS
NEGATIVE EMOTIONS

Use your mind to find reasons not to express negative emotions. One of the ways that you can do this is to first say, "I am responsible!" and then look into the situation for examples and reasons in which you might be responsible in some way for what has happened.

People who go through bad relationships are often furious at the other person, sometimes for years, when the relationship or marriage breaks down. But when you say, "I am responsible!" and look for reasons why this may be so, you will find that you made a lot of the decisions that got you into the bad relationship in the first place. You may not be totally responsible for the actions of the other person, but you are fully responsible for everything you did or said from the beginning of the relationship to the end, and to the present day.

Many people become upset over a job or a business deal that goes wrong. But you are responsible. No one forced you into the situation at gunpoint. Based on your knowledge and information, or lack of knowledge, you got yourself into the situation in the first place. It did not work out as you expected. Next time you will be smarter and wiser. But for the moment, you are responsible.

THE LAW OF EMOTION

The *law of emotion* says that everything you do is determined by an emotion of some kind, either positive or negative. The emotions that you think about and talk about the most soon grow and consume your entire life, for better or worse.

Imagine that you have two fires burning. One is the fire of desire and the other is the fire of negative emotions, based on your interpretation of past events. You have a load of emotional firewood. You can put this wood on either fire. But if you put all the wood on one fire, what happens to the other fire?

The answer is simple. If you put all of your emotions on the fire of desire, and spend all your time thinking and talking about what you want and where you are going with your life, the old fire of negative emotions and experiences eventually dies out and the ashes go cold. This is the bottom line of all emotional healing.

From now on, when something goes wrong, for any reason, immediately say, "I am responsible!" and stop the negative emotion from getting started in the first place.

Your Great Goal

Aristotle was perhaps the greatest of the ancient philosophers. One of his major contributions was his discovery of what he thought to be the ultimate ends or goals of human behavior. He said that behind everything we do, there is another motivation, until we get back to the core motivation of all human behavior, which is to be happy.

You are a happiness-seeking organism. Your primary aim in life is to be happy, however you define it. And the very best measure of happiness is how much peace of mind you enjoy, and how often you enjoy it.

Peace of mind is the highest human good. The very best moments of your life are those when you feel completely at peace with yourself, with other people, and with the world. Your goal is to do everything possible to achieve and attain these feelings of peace and happiness. When you do this, everything in your life tends to work out for the better.

EXERCISE: Think of the times when you felt the most content, happy and relaxed. Where were you? Whom were you with? What was it about the situation that made you happy? How could you duplicate that experience on a regular basis?

Locus of Control

There are more than fifty years of research into what is called *locus of control* theory. In these studies, people are divided into two categories, those who have an *internal* locus of control and those who have an *external* locus of control.

An internal locus of control is experienced when the individual feels that she is in complete charge of her thoughts, feelings, and behaviors. An internal locus of control is closely associated with happiness, optimism, high energy, good health, positive relationships, and success in life.

An external locus of control is experienced when the individual feels that he has little or no control over his life, that he is controlled by other people or circumstances. An external locus of control is closely associated with feelings of distress, depression, frustration, helplessness, and inferiority.

People with an external locus of control tend to feel negative, pessimistic, and angry. They are more susceptible to psychosomatic illnesses, depression, and problems in relationships.

Whenever you are blaming someone else for something in your life, you are giving that person control over your emotions.

You are giving up your peace of mind to that other person. You are putting that other person, rather than yourself, in control of your happiness.

TAKE CONTROL OF YOUR EMOTIONS

The key to developing an internal locus of control, to taking complete charge of yourself and your life, is to firmly state, "I am responsible!" whenever you feel like lashing out or blaming someone else for anything.

There is a direct relationship between the amount of responsibility you accept for yourself, your feelings, and your life and the amount of control you feel you have over what happens to you. At the same time, there is a direct relationship between how much control you feel you have and positive emotions. Finally, there is a direct relationship between responsibility, control, and positive emotions on the one hand, and how happy you feel on the other hand.

The more you accept responsibility for every part of your life, the happier, more positive, and more optimistic you will feel. Your mental, physical, and emotional energies will be directed outward on accomplishment, on making your life into something wonderful, and on realizing your full potential.

Shed Feelings of Guilt and Unworthiness

There is a special area of personal negativity that holds you back from becoming everything you are capable of becoming, and that is *feelings of guilt*.

Children are born with no feelings of guilt. Every guilty feeling that you experience as an adult was taught to you by your parents, siblings, and others as you were growing up. And because feelings of guilt have been learned, they can be unlearned as well.

Parents usually use guilt on their children because it was used on them by *their* parents, and often by their grandparents. The practice of guilt throwing goes back through the generations. It almost becomes automatic with some people, and in some families and religions.

THE IMPACT OF "NEGATIVE RELIGION"

There are churches that practice what I call *negative religion*. In these churches, and certain other schools of thought, including large aspects of socialism and communism, guilt is used systematically and deliberately to undermine positive emotions, destroy personalities, and make people easily controllable by the person who is casting the guilt on everyone else.

When guilt is practiced deliberately, it is used for two purposes: *control* and *manipulation*. Throughout the centuries, people and parents have found that if you can make others feel guilty about something, you can easily control their emotions. If you can control their emotions, you can then manipulate them into doing or not doing what you want. Guilt is an insidious and evil emotion used exclusively to get people to do what the guilt inducer wants by destroying their sense of self-worth and lowering their resistance to being controlled by others.

THE HARM OF WITHHOLDING LOVE

In an earlier section, we touched upon how children frequently become susceptible to feelings of constant guilt as the result of destructive criticism or lack of love they experience early in their

lives, often at the hands of their parents, siblings, or other authority figures they trust. When children are told that they are no
good or stupid, a disappointment to their parents, or not very
smart or competent, they naturally begin to develop feelings of
unworthiness and inferiority. They think to themselves the destructive words "I'm not good enough" and "It must be my fault."

When children are continually criticized as they are growing
up, they soon begin to criticize themselves. This self-criticism
manifests in negative comparisons with others. All around them
they see people who are doing better than they are, whether it is
in sports, academics, or social activities, and they feel guilty for
not being as able as their peers in all aspects of their lives. Because
they have feelings of inferiority, they conclude naturally that if
someone is *doing* better than they are in a specific area, that person
must therefore *be* better than they are as well.

FROM WORTH LESS TO *WORTHLESS*

After negatively comparing oneself with others for so long, the
guilt-ridden person concludes, "If someone else is doing 'better'
than I am, that person must be worth more than I am. If that
person is worth more, than I must be worth less. And it's only a
small step from thinking you are worth less than someone else to
believing you are *worthless* entirely.

For this reason, feelings of guilt almost inevitably lead to
feelings of worthlessness. A person who feels worthless, dimin-
ished, and of little value becomes insecure, pessimistic, angry, and
dissatisfied.

Among the prison population today, for example, the worst
offenders, and those serving the longest terms, have zero sense of

responsibility and zero self-esteem. Many of them can clearly remember their fathers or mothers telling them things such as, "You are no good; someday you will end up in prison."

Feelings of guilt and inferiority lead very quickly to a person seeing herself as a victim—of life, circumstances, fate, society, and numerous other factors. This feeling is expressed in the words "I'm not good enough." The individual continually compares herself with others and says, "I am not smart enough," "I'm not talented enough," "I'm not competent enough," "I'm no good," "I can't! I can't! I can't!"

Feeling guilty also often leads to needing to take care of someone else's needs or feelings before taking care of your own. People seek out permission or approval before making a decision.

GUILT THROWERS AND GUILT CATCHERS

For more than two thousand years, guilt has been a fundamental principle in Judeo-Christian culture. It has been used over the centuries for manipulation and control of individuals and populations who have been made to feel guilty. Guilt is useful in soliciting charitable or religious contributions and eliciting obedience.

Much of society is made up of people who are *guilt throwers* and those who are *guilt catchers*. Guilt throwers have mastered the ability to make people, often complete strangers, feel guilty in just a few seconds. Guilt catchers are easily made to feel guilty by guilt throwers. Since opposites often attract in the area of temperament, many little guilt throwers grow up and marry guilt catchers, repeating their family dynamic as adults.

EXERCISE: If you can't directly confront someone who makes you feel guilty, try sitting in front of an empty chair and imagine that the other person is sitting there. Tell him how you feel and that you refuse to feel guilty anymore. Tell him that he will now have to assume responsibility for his own life, feelings, and experiences. You are going to take care of yourself. If it helps, put a picture of the person on the other chair. Or you can even ask a friend or partner to role-play with you.

Avoid the "Victim Language" Trap

Once a person develops feelings of guilt, unworthiness, and inferiority, he or she continues to reinforce those feelings by using victim language. The majority of what you think and feel about yourself is determined by the way you talk to yourself, your "inner dialogue," throughout the day. The inner dialogue of guilt-ridden people who see themselves as victims is full of complaining, criticizing, and blaming others.

People who feel like victims continually *make excuses*. When you ask them for something, they often say, "I'll try," or "I'll do my best," which is essentially an excuse for failure, in advance. It's not remotely empowering or motivating for a person who feels like a victim, and it induces serious doubt and distrust in the person who's making the request. Whenever someone says these words when you ask them to do something, you know that they likely are going to fail and disappoint. And they know it too. They are continually offering up justifications and explanations for not trying, not achieving goals, not being punctual, not fulfilling their responsibilities, and not doing the job that they were hired to do. They always have a reason or an excuse, because they always see themselves as a victim. Nothing is ever their fault.

This also means they have no ownership of their ability to succeed and no control over the outcome of anything they attempt. By assuming they will fail before they even try, they are creating a self-fulfilling prophecy that makes it all but impossible to achieve what they want or what they need to do. Achievers do the opposite: They believe they will achieve successful results and then they go after them. You can't succeed if you don't even try.

Criticizing and complaining are usually forms of victim language as well. When you criticize and complain, you position yourself as a victim of those about whom you are criticizing and complaining in the first place. As a result, this makes you feel inferior and insecure.

Eliminate Feelings of Guilt

There are four steps that you can take to unlearn the feelings of guilt that may have been programmed into you from an early age:

1. **From this moment on, never criticize yourself for anything.** Practice self-compassion. Never say anything to yourself about yourself that you do not sincerely want to be true. Remember, the most powerful words in your vocabulary are those you say to yourself and believe. Make sure that they are positive and upbeat.

The very best words that you can say to yourself, over and over, are "I like myself!" "I can do it!" and "I am responsible!" It is impossible to repeat these affirmations and feel negative or guilty at the same time.

2. **Refuse to criticize anyone else for anything that they do or say.** Eliminate destructive criticism from your vocabulary altogether. Be the kind of person from whom "never is heard a discouraging word."

   Make it a habit to be curious and to continually seek out positive things in other people and comment on them. Whenever you say anything nice to another person, for any reason, you raise his or her self-esteem, and your own self-esteem goes up in equal measure.

3. **Refuse to use guilt on other people, for any reason.** Abolish the use of guilt-laden words and phrases from your vocabulary and from your interactions with your family and friends. Never try to make a person feel guilty for something that he or she has done or not done.

   The greatest gifts you can give another person are those of *unconditional love* and *acceptance*. This means that you never criticize her for anything that she does or doesn't do. You praise, approve, or at the very least remain silent.

4. **Refuse to be manipulated by guilt coming from someone else.** From this day forward, reject any attempt to make you feel guilty for any reason.

   If your mother, father, or spouse tries to make you feel guilty, simply ask, "You're not trying to make me feel guilty, are you?" and remain silent.

Very few people will admit outright that they are attempting to manipulate another person by using guilt.
They will say something like, "Of course not."

If you ask, "Are you trying to make me feel guilty?"
and the other person responds, "Yes, I am," you simply
say, "Well, it's not going to work."

It is absolutely amazing what happens when you tell
people who are accustomed to manipulating you by using
guilt that it's not going to work anymore. They may be
angry and confused at first. But as they realize that the
throwing of guilt has no effect on your behavior, they will
begin to change and communicate with you in a more
positive way. Try it and see.

Your great goal in life must be the elimination of negative
emotions, of all kinds. In the absence of negative emotions, only
positive emotions will fill your mind. The two most powerful
positive emotion builders are the phrases "I like myself!" and "I
am responsible!" Say them repeatedly.

The more you like yourself, the more responsibility you
accept. The more responsibility you accept, the more you like
yourself. Each feeds on and reinforces the other.

Discover Your Meaning and Purpose

Viktor Frankl, the founder of logotherapy and the author of the
book *Man's Search for Meaning*, said that the need for meaning and
purpose is the deepest of our motivations.

True meaning and purpose come only when you are busy

doing something that makes a difference in the lives of other people.

There is a direct relationship between your level of self-esteem (how much you like yourself) and how much you feel that you are making a contribution to your world. People who feel they are making a difference, that they are putting in more than they are taking out, feel happy, strong, and very much in control of their lives.

The only real antidote to negative emotions, worry, fear, and guilt is to get so busy doing something that you enjoy, and that benefits others in some way, that you no longer have any time to think about things that might have made you unhappy in the past.

Motivational radio host and author of *The Strangest Secret*, Earl Nightingale once said, "Happiness is the progressive realization of a worthy ideal."

True happiness, positive emotions, and feelings of optimism and elation come when you feel that you are moving step by step in the direction of doing, being, and accomplishing something important in your life.

When you eliminate the negative emotions, all that is left are the positive emotions. Fortunately, you can unlearn negative emotions with practice. Then only positive emotions will grow and eventually guide and direct everything you do.

✦ ✦ ✦

CHAPTER THREE

Letting Go of the Past

In the final analysis, the question of why bad things happen to good people transmutes itself into some very different questions, no longer asking why something happened, but asking how we will respond, what we intend to do now that it has happened.

—HAROLD S. KUSHNER

Your goal in life is to be happy, joyous, and free as much of the time as you possibly can. Your aim must be to get rid of all the old baggage and negativity that holds you back, like a lead weight, and stops you from achieving all that is possible for you.

Perhaps the most important principle of success and happiness is contained in the *law of forgiveness*: You are mentally healthy to the degree to which you can freely forgive, forget, and let go of any negative experience.

Almost all the great religions teach the importance of forgiveness as the key to the spiritual kingdom. If you cannot forgive, you are locked in place. You cannot make any progress. You are held back year after year by your refusal or unwillingness to let go of a previous hurt.

Three Mental Laws

The *law of emotion* says that everything you do is motivated by an emotion of one kind or another, positive or negative. You can hold only one thought in your conscious mind at a time, positive or negative, and you are always *free to choose.*

The *law of habit* says that whatever you do repeatedly eventually becomes a new habit. The rule is that good habits are hard to form but easy to live with. Bad habits, especially emotional reactions, are easy to form but hard to live with. The majority of what you do, think, say, or feel is determined by habit, either good or bad.

The *law of substitution* says that you can substitute a positive thought for a negative thought. You can deliberately decide to think a thought that makes you positive or happy as a substitute for any thought that makes you unhappy.

Two Brain Mechanisms

But here is the kicker: You have both a *success mechanism* and a *failure mechanism* in your brain. The success mechanism is activated when you think positive, loving, forgiving thoughts about yourself and other people and focus on your goals. These thoughts require conscious, continuous, deliberate effort on your part. They do not happen by accident, but by design.

Your failure mechanism, unfortunately, works automatically when you stop thinking about what you want and the things that make you happy. Your failure mechanism is a "default setting" that is activated as soon as you stop thinking positive, constructive thoughts.

This means that if you do not deliberately choose to think thoughts that make you happy, your mind defaults to negative thoughts that make you unhappy. Fortunately, by the law of habit, if you discipline yourself to keep your mind on positive thoughts, it eventually becomes a habit. When positive thinking becomes a habit, it becomes your "automatic setting," and you begin to perform at your best at home and at work.

Unhappy Today Because of Yesterday

The primary reason that people are unhappy today is because they are still angry with someone who did or did not do something to them or for them in the past. They still have not forgiven another person for a mistake they feel that person made or a wrong they feel that person inflicted upon them. Here are a few common sources of past anger or hurt that can still affect you today.

PARENTS AND CHILDREN

When you are a child, your parents take care of everything. They feed you, bathe you, clothe you, take you to school, pick you up, and watch over you. At an early age, most children get the feeling that they are surrounded by the arms of a protector who is all-knowing, all-powerful, and all-wise. As a result, children come to expect that they live in a rational, logical, and orderly universe where their all-knowing parents care for them, protect them, and make the best decisions for them.

According to Jean Piaget, the Swiss psychologist and child development specialist who wrote *The Construction of Reality in the*

Child, children evolve and mature, moving upward through ever-complex levels of understanding in human interaction. At one of these levels, early in life, children expect everything to be fair and just. If for any reason they see or experience what they consider to be injustice in their world, they can become angry or disappointed, feelings that can carry on into their adult lives.

FRUSTRATED EXPECTATIONS

Many negative emotions also arise from *frustrated expectations* over past events. This means that a person expected things to happen a certain way, and for whatever reason, things turned out differently than anticipated—and not in a good way (at least according to the person experiencing the frustrated expectations). As a result, the individual feels angry and disappointed. She lashes out and demands that her expectations be fulfilled. If the situation is not corrected to her liking, she becomes angrier and even more frustrated.

Becoming attached to the outcome of a situation is quite normal. Often, based on information we collect and actions we take, we expect things to turn out a certain way. By determining our desired outcome in advance and taking steps to achieve it, we have a sense of control. We can plan what is often an unknowable future. It is when our expectations are frustrated by not getting the outcome we hoped for or strived to meet that we become angry or depressed.

A WORD FROM CHRISTINA

I once worked with a couple whose biggest source of contention was her need and expectation for him to arrive home from work at the precise time he said he would be home. She viewed time in a very literal and precise way and would make preparations for the exact time that he would give her. On the contrary, her husband thought about time as a range. He would say he would be home at seven o'clock—to her that meant exactly seven o'clock; to him it meant between seven and eight, depending on when he could actually leave work.

He would say he'd be home by seven, and based on past experience, she would expect him to be late. She then would begin to feel angry and frustrated, assuming he didn't care enough about her to be on time. She took his tardiness as a personal insult. He then would arrive home to an unhappy wife, and a heated disagreement would ensue. This cycle continued for months.

In working with them, I helped them to understand each other's ideas about timing. I helped her to understand that she needed to accept his range approach so that she could change her expectations and stop setting herself up for disappointment, and I emphasized to him that his insistence on citing a specific time for when he would be home was understandably hurting his wife's feelings, and he needed to give her a range instead.

When they managed to do these things, it completely changed the quality of their relationship. She could still plan for his arrival, but accept that his timing was more flexible than she had previously understood. In turn, he became more punctual and looked forward to coming home and seeing her as opposed to dragging his feet, dreading the daily battle.

Bounce Back

A good way to bounce back from any situation that does not turn out the way you expected is for you *look for the good* in the unexpected outcome. You can always find something positive and beneficial, and while you are searching, you will remain calm and positive.

EXERCISE: Look into a current situation in your life that is making you mad or sad. What is good in this situation? Napoleon Hill wrote, "Within every problem or difficulty there lies the seed of an equal or greater advantage or benefit." What could that seed be for you?

Remain Flexible

Stay flexible. Be open to the fact that things do not always turn out exactly as you expected. Keep your mind open.

As children grow and develop, they learn that life is not black and white, but many shades of gray. Sometimes things work out well, and sometimes they don't. Life is a series of ups and downs, in which sometimes parents make the right decisions and sometimes they don't.

However, many children fixate at a particular level of development, expecting and then demanding that life be fair, just, consistent, and predictable. Once fixated at this level, they can grow into adults who still demand that life be consistent and predictable. When it is not, they become angry, frustrated, and often depressed.

Another way to increase your flexibility is to lower your expectations of a situation that typically causes you frustration. You can actually set the situation up to be a success and enjoyable for you by doing this.

For example, I work with a lot of women who are balancing motherhood and a profession. These women often attempt to accomplish too much throughout the day, and when there are things left undone or incomplete at the end of the day, they feel dissatisfied with themselves and their results for that day. The solution to this self-induced pressure is for you not to take on more work than you can get done in the time you have available.

Human Imperfection

The fact is that human beings are imperfect. You are imperfect. I am imperfect. Every individual and every organization consisting of individuals is imperfect. People make mistakes. They do wicked, senseless, brainless, foolish, and cruel things. This is the way the world is and has always been. To expect everything to be fine all the time is to court eternal frustration and doubt. And yet, unconsciously, many people go through life expecting that all will be well.

Many people, while growing up, get the idea that the world is supposed to unfold in a particular way. If it does not, instead of adjusting and adapting, they become angry, frustrated, and determined either to impose their will on their world or make other people behave in a way more in harmony with what they have come to expect. This attitude is a major motivator of political activity.

The Miracle of Forgiveness

The decision to practice forgiveness as an ongoing policy in life is essential in moving from being a child to being an adult. When you forgive, you free yourself from negative emotions and guilt, and you free other people as well. You move from victim to victor. You free yourself from the baggage of the past and unleash your potential for realizing your future.

"Let it go, let it go, let it go. . . ."

Forgiveness is the key. Your ability to freely forgive other people is the mark of your development as a fully functioning person. The greatest souls of the ages have been those who have developed themselves to the point where they hold no animosity toward anyone, for any reason. Your goal should be the same. The practice of forgiveness is your key to becoming everything you are capable of becoming.

THE COMMON ERROR

Some people think it is not possible to forgive. They are convinced that forgiving another person is the same as approving of his behavior or condoning the unkind or cruel thing he has done.

They feel that by forgiving, they are actually letting the other person off the hook, letting him go free when it is clear that he has done or said something harmful or hurtful.

But here is the key: Forgiveness has nothing to do with the other person. Forgiveness has only to do with *you*. It is a perfectly selfish act. By forgiving the other person, you do not set him free; you set yourself free.

The comedian Buddy Hackett once said, "I never hold grudges; while you're holding grudges, they're out dancing."

It is said that most of our problems in life come with hair on top, and talk back. Almost all your negative emotions, especially those of anger and guilt, are associated with another person or persons. When I ask my clients, "What is the biggest problem, worry, or concern in your life today?" the answer almost always comes back as another person or persons.

Green Buttons and Red Buttons

My friend Jim Newman conducted a three-day seminar on personal growth and effectiveness for many years. Part of the seminar involved imagining a series of red buttons and green buttons on your chest. Whenever someone pushes one of your green buttons, you smile and are happy. Whenever someone pushes one of your red buttons, you become angry and want to strike out.

The green buttons are happy memories and associations with people in your life whom you love and enjoy, such as your spouse or children. The red buttons are attached to memories of people who have hurt you, and whom you automatically feel angry about when their name is mentioned, or even when something reminds you of them.

CONSCIOUSLY REWIRE YOUR BUTTONS

What Jim taught was that the key to taking complete control of your emotions is to rewire your buttons. The way you do this is by reprogramming yourself to think a positive thought rather than a negative thought whenever one of your red buttons is pushed. When you do this repeatedly, the negativity associated with that other person becomes weaker and weaker, and eventually disappears.

Here is a simple statement that you can repeat whenever the unhappy memory of that person is triggered: "God bless him/her; I forgive him/her and wish him/her well." And then just let it go, and get your mind busy elsewhere.

Because your emotions operate at such an incredible speed, it is not possible to gain control of them at the moment that they are triggered by a negative memory. You must program them in advance. You do this by saying, "Whenever I think of that person, I will bless, forgive, and let go."

SIMPLE PSYCHOLOGY

You can think only one thought at a time. When you deliberately think a positive thought, all negative thoughts stop instantly. If you keep thinking positive thoughts, though it may be difficult at the beginning, by the law of habit, it soon becomes automatic and easy.

It is not possible to remain angry with someone if you bless him, forgive him, and wish him well. As you repeat these words, over and over, you will eventually find that when that red button is pushed, it has been disconnected from your emotions. Whereas before, the thought or image made you angry, now your response is completely neutral. You feel nothing at all. Soon you actually forget about the person or situation completely. It's quite amazing, and sometimes life changing.

THE KEY TO HAPPINESS

The practice of forgiveness is the key to your happiness. From now on, when you think of someone who still makes you unhappy, use your wonderful intelligence to think of reasons to forgive and let go.

Instead of reminding yourself of the unkind things that person did to hurt you, you bless, forgive, and let go. Soon this response becomes a habit, and your whole personality changes for the better.

EXERCISE: Make a list of three to five people you are still angry with. Think about each person and then say to yourself, "I choose to let go of this situation and I forgive him/her for everything."

The Process of Forgiveness

When we explain the importance of forgiveness in our seminars, almost everyone agrees that it is a good policy. They all nod, smile, and agree that in the future, they are going to freely forgive others who have hurt them, and let them go. But when we come to the specific people they need to forgive, the emotional blocks appear.

FOUR PEOPLE TO FORGIVE

There are four people you must learn to forgive if you truly want to be happy: your parents, your past relationships, everyone else, and most important, yourself.

1. Your Parents

The first people you have to forgive are your parents. Most adults are still angry about something that one of their parents did or did not do to them or for them while they were growing up. They expected their parents to behave in a certain way, and their parents did something different. The adult children are still angry today, often after many years.

At a seminar in Orlando, Florida, I had lunch with one of my participants, a man named Bill. He told me about his ex-wife, whom he had divorced after more than twenty years. She had been negative, angry, and complaining the entire time, and finally he'd had enough. He wasn't willing to spend the rest of his life with that kind of person.

As he told me his story, he mentioned having lunch with his ex-wife the previous week. Because they had two children, they had to meet and talk occasionally. At this luncheon, he told her that he was concerned about her negativity, and how she seemed to continually criticize and complain about other people and situations.

She reacted by saying, "Well, you'd be negative too if your mother had treated you the way my mother treated me when I was a teenager."

Bill said, "Susan, you haven't lived with your mother for more than twenty-five years. How long are you going to use her as an excuse for your problems as an adult?"

There are many people who are locked in place emotionally, still angry at one or both parents for injuries or hurts that happened many years ago. Sometimes, people are still angry with their parents long after their parents have died. As a result, they remain as children in their own minds, see themselves as victims, feel angry and frustrated, and often take out their anger on their own spouses and children.

The first people you have to forgive are your parents. Whether they are living or dead, in the same city or living far away, you must freely forgive your parents for everything they did or said that hurt you in any way while you were growing up.

You must say, "God bless them. I forgive them and I wish them well."

Here is a key point: Your parents did the very best they could with you, with who they were and what they had. They were products of their own childhood and upbringing. Their parents were in turn products of their upbringing by their own parents. In each case, they could not have done other than what they did. They could not have raised their children differently. They simply did not know how.

Just as you are not perfect, your parents were not perfect either. They had fears and doubts, just as you do. They made mistakes and did silly, wicked, foolish, cruel, and brainless things. They brought you into the world with the very best of intentions and did the best they could with what they knew.

Whenever you remember something your parents did that hurt you, remind yourself that if they knew that they had said or done something that caused you pain in any way, they would probably feel terrible about it. In most cases, parents would never do something intentionally to hurt their children. If you have children, imagine how you would feel if your child told you that you had hurt them in some way. You would never intentionally cause pain to your child. Neither would your parents.

Now you have to forgive them completely for every mistake they ever made in bringing you up. You have to let them off the hook. You have to set them free. Because only in setting your parents free through the practice of forgiveness can you set yourself free as well. Only by letting them off the hook do you let yourself off the hook. Only by forgiving your parents do you become a fully functioning adult.

One of my seminar participants went to his father's home after the seminar in which he learned these principles. He told me later that, at the age of thirty-five, he was still furious about something his father had done when he was fifteen years old. This brooding anger was affecting his relationship with his wife and children. He had to get it off his chest, so he went directly to his father's home from the seminar.

His heart was pounding, but he went straight up to his father and said, "Dad, do you remember when I was fifteen and you did that thing? I just want you to know that I forgive you completely for that, and for every mistake you ever made in bringing me up. And I love you."

His father was a gruff, stern workingman. He looked the son in the eye and said in an irritated tone of voice, "I have no idea what you're talking about. I have never done anything in my life that I need to be forgiven for by you."

He looked at his father with shock. He was stunned. He suddenly realized that he had been angry and upset for twenty years about something his father never even knew that he had done. He shook his head, shook hands with his father, and said good-bye. He walked out into the night feeling as if a huge burden had been lifted off his shoulders.

EXERCISE: If your relationship with your parents was particularly bad, you may want to sit down and write a letter, spelling out every single thing that you can remember that caused you unhappiness or grief when you were growing up. You can start the letter by writing, "I want to forgive you for the following things that you did that hurt me when I was growing up." At the end of the letter, finish by writing, "I forgive you for everything. I love you and I wish you well."

EXERCISE: If you are in contact with your parents, it may also be healing to sit down with them and explore the motivation behind something they said or did. Why did they do or say a particular thing? This can help you alter your perspective on the situation. Often if you understand what was going on in your parents' minds at the time, you can completely change the way you feel about an experience. The key to making this work is that you must approach the discussion in a low-key, curious, and positive way. Be careful not to make your parents feel that you are attacking them. This will only make them defensive.

A WORD FROM CHRISTINA

I have a friend who has always felt that her parents loved her sister more than they loved her. They treated her sister very differently and had a closer relationship with her. From childhood, my friend was aware of this difference.

As she grew up, she felt that she had to work harder for acknowledgment and acceptance from her parents and was not given as many privileges as her sister. As the years went by, she felt more and more hurt, always wondering what was wrong with her and why her parents did not love the two children equally.

One night, she finally decided to confront them and ask why they continued to do certain things for her sister and not for her. What had she done to make them love her less?

They responded with shock and surprise at the thought that they had treated the two girls differently. They were both absolutely convinced that they treated each child the same. They did not understand my friend's perspective. She came home that night realizing that her parents would never change or even agree that they treated the two girls differently. Nonetheless, she felt liberated and relieved to have expressed her feelings to her parents. They did not accept her feelings, but they did hear her, and that was all she needed.

Once you have forgiven your parents, you will have made a giant stride forward. You will have done something that few people ever do in their entire lives. The very act of forgiving your parents will begin the process of personal liberation. You will already start to feel happier and at peace, even before you do it.

2. Past Relationships

The second group of people you must forgive are all those in your past relationships, your romances, and your ex-spouses. Personal, intimate relationships make us very vulnerable to the way people treat us. We say and do things in the throes of love and passion that open us up and expose us to the other person. We give our minds, hearts, and bodies in some of the most intense moments of our lives.

When a romantic relationship does not work out and falls apart, we are often overwhelmed by negative emotions. We feel anger and guilt. We experience envy and resentment. We justify and rationalize. We blame, criticize, and condemn. If we don't get our emotions under control, we can experience a mild or even a major form of insanity. We feel as if our whole emotional lives are plunged into a black hole.

But here again, you must use your wonderful mind to defuse these negative emotions, to resolve the situation in some way and get on with the rest of your life.

The fact is, no one can have any control over your emotions unless there is still something that you want from him or her.

In psychology, this is called the *incomplete action*. We are often angry and upset over a past relationship because there are one or more issues that have not yet been resolved.

The worst of all is probably when one person is still in love and wants the other person to love him or her back. However, if the other person has moved on emotionally and has no more romantic interest in the past partner, the person who has been left behind emotionally can experience incredibly complicated feelings of anger, guilt, unworthiness, undeservingness, unattractiveness, and inferiority.

The way to practice forgiveness in a past relationship is to accept responsibility for what happened or didn't happen. Instead of blaming the other person for what he or she did or didn't do, you must accept that you are equally responsible for getting yourself into the relationship and keeping yourself in it. In many cases, you probably knew that it was the wrong relationship to get into in the first place, and you probably knew that you should have gotten out a long time ago.

In a study of several thousand married couples who had gone for premarital counseling, 38 percent of them, one or the other, admitted that they did not want to marry the other person. They felt it was a mistake. But they went through with the marriage ceremony anyway because they felt that their family and friends were expecting them to get married.

The moral of the story is: Never stay in a bad relationship out of fear of what others, especially your friends and family members, may think, feel, or say if you were to separate. Never do or refrain from doing something because you are worried about what other people might think about you. You will eventually learn that *nobody was ever thinking about you at all.* In fact, if you knew how little other people think about you, you would probably be insulted. Your whole romantic life could be going down the drain and other people are only thinking about what they are going to have for lunch.

It's OK to be a little selfish and put your own happiness first. Do only what you feel is the right thing to do for you. Never allow yourself to be influenced by the positive or negative opinions of others. Please at least yourself in all things, if you can't please everyone else too.

Many people will go through a bad marriage and divorce, and will still be upset and angry ten and twenty years later. They still blame the other person for the marriage not having worked out. They cannot let go of the fact that the marriage, into which they had invested so much, had failed. They still cannot forgive the other person for the things that he or she did or didn't do.

But just as with parenting, when people get married, they do the best that they know how. No one enters into a marriage with the intention of it failing. They always enter into it with the very best hopes, dreams, and aspirations. If later, in the fullness of time, the people change and the marriage doesn't work out, it is not the fault of either party.

In the movie *Good Will Hunting*, the critical point in the relationship between Matt Damon's character, Will, and Robin Williams's character, Sean, Will's psychologist, comes after Will has explained the traumatic experiences of his youth. Sean says to him, "It's not your fault."

This part of the movie is very moving and revealing. Will says, "Sure, sure, I know." Again, Sean says, "It's not your fault. It's not your fault. It's not your fault." Finally, Will understands what Sean is saying. No matter what happened in his childhood, however traumatic it was, it was not his fault. At that moment he is free at last.

In an unhappy marriage, it's not your fault either; nor is it the fault of the other person. The two people, who were once compatible enough to marry, are now no longer compatible. Incompatibility is not a choice. It is like the weather. It just happens. The two people drift apart and have different thoughts, feelings, and ideas about themselves, their lives, their work, their children, and their place in society. It is no one's fault.

If you are in a situation in which you are still angry about a relationship or marriage that did not succeed, you must first decide in your own mind to let it go. As long as you cling to the hope that it will somehow come back together, you can never be free. You can never get on with your life. You can never be happy.

EXERCISE: WRITE THE LETTER: Once you have let it go, sit down and write "the Letter." This is one of the most powerful tools that you can use to set yourself free and achieve lasting happiness and peace of mind.

This is what you do: Take a piece of paper and begin writing the letter, addressing the other person. Your opening paragraph reads, "It is unfortunate that our marriage did not succeed. However, I accept complete responsibility for my role in the marriage, and everything I did or didn't do that led to its failure."

Continue with "I forgive you for everything you did or said that hurt me." (At this point, many people make a list of every single thing they can think of that the other person ever did that still makes them angry when they think about it.)

The last line is simply: "I wish you well."

Take this letter, seal it in an envelope, put the correct address and postage on the envelope, and drop it into the mailbox.

The instant your hand lets go of this letter and you know that it is irretrievable, you will feel as though an enormous burden has been lifted off you. You will feel happy and relaxed. You will smile and feel at peace.

At this point, people will often say, "But what if the other person misinterprets the letter and wants to get back together again?"

The answer is simple: Don't worry. You are not writing this letter for the other person. You are writing this letter for yourself. As far as the other person is concerned, you don't care if he or she is happy or unhappy, angry or upset, pleased or displeased. You simply do not care. It is over. You are free at last.

In many cases, when one person has the courage to accept responsibility and forgive the other person for everything that happened, the other person changes completely, losing all his or her animosity. All the negative emotions drain out of the memory of their relationship. Many former couples have told me that after one wrote this letter, the two became good friends and were able to be excellent parents to their children.

If the act of mailing the letter is too intimidating for you, you can write the letter and instead rip it up and throw it away. But the mailing of the letter is the cathartic event that makes the forgiveness irreversible.

3. Everyone Else

The third group of people you have to forgive is everyone else in your life who has ever hurt you in any way. You have to forgive your siblings, who may have been unkind to you when you were growing up. You have to forgive your friends of all ages who may have done unkind or cruel things to you. You have to forgive your previous employers who may have treated you poorly or fired you unjustly.

You have to forgive your business partners and associates who may have cheated you or cost you money. You have to forgive every person you can think of in any part of your life for whom you still hold anger and still blame for something he or she did.

Remember, you are not forgiving all of these people for themselves. You are forgiving them for *yourself*. You do not even have to tell the other person that you have forgiven her. You can simply forgive her in your heart. Whenever you think of the other person, you quickly cancel the negative thought by saying, "God bless her; I forgive her and wish her well."

Whenever a negative thought of that other person comes into your mind, immediately cancel it by blessing her and wishing her well. Refuse to discuss the other person or situation with others. This simply heaps fuel on the fire and delays the healing process. Instead, cancel the thought and blot it out of your mind. Eventually, you will think of that person less and less, and then you will forget her completely. You will not think of her at all.

There are only two times of your life, the past and the future. The present is a fleeting moment between the two. One of the most important decisions you will ever make is to never allow yourself to be angry or unhappy about something you can't change, and you cannot change the past. It is over. It is gone. It is irreversible. But the future can be changed. It is under your control, and it is determined by what you do in the present.

Imagine that you run into a man at a social function and ask him, "How are you doing?" He replies with a sour look and says something like, "I am doing fine, but I am still really angry about what happened."

A bit surprised, you ask, "What happened?"

He goes on to say, "Well, about five years ago, my family and I packed a picnic basket on Saturday night so that we could go out and have a nice picnic on Sunday. But on Sunday morning, it was overcast and raining for the whole day so we had to cancel the picnic. And I'm still mad."

At about this time, you would probably be thinking, "This person needs a checkup from the neck up. He is not playing with a full deck. He is not thinking rationally. How could a person still be angry about the fact that it *rained* five years ago? This is ridiculous!"

Here is my point: Many people are still miserable and unhappy today because of something that happened or didn't happen years ago. They can't let it go. It may have been a difficult childhood. It could have been a bad marriage. It might have been a lousy job or a poor investment. But whatever it is, because of their inability to forgive and let go, they are trapped, like the dinosaurs in the tar pits, year after year.

If you have led a normal life, you have made all kinds of mistakes and had all kinds of problems with all kinds of people over the years, starting from early childhood. This is normal and natural and a part of the human experience. The only question is,

"Do you rise above it by practicing forgiveness early and often, or do you let it weigh you down and hold you back?"

Many people will agree by now that they should and will forgive all those people who have hurt them in the past. But at the same time, almost like a card player holding a card close to his chest, they carve out a single area of unforgivingness. They decide that they will forgive everybody they can think of, but there is one person who hurt them so much that he or she cannot be allowed to go free.

But by holding on to this one negative emotion, the refusal to forgive this one person or what happened in that situation is enough to sabotage all your hopes and dreams for health, happiness, and personal fulfillment. One negative emotion that you hold on to can undermine all your hopes for happiness and joy in the future.

4. Finally, Set Yourself Free

The fourth person you must forgive is *yourself*. Now that you have had the courage and character to forgive everyone in your life who has ever hurt you, you must forgive yourself and let yourself off the hook, as well.

Many people are held back all their lives because of a mistake they made in years past. Perhaps you did something wicked, brainless, or cruel when you were growing up. Perhaps you hurt someone in an early relationship. Perhaps you did something that caused a good deal of pain, money, and unhappiness to someone in work or business.

Today, you feel remorse and regret. You feel unhappy and

burdened. You wish you had not done or said what you did. You feel guilty and negative. These feelings can hold you back, like weights, from rising to fulfill your complete potential. They can be like that brake on the front wheel that is locked in place, causing your life to go in circles.

Here is a key point: The person you are today and the person who did or said those things in the past are not one and the same. You are different today, wiser and more experienced, someone who would never do the thing that the person you were in the past did at that time. You cannot continue to punish who you are today by continually regretting what you did when you were a different person, a long time ago.

Regret and remorse are not signs of responsibility or conscience. They are actually weaknesses that hold you back.

Say to yourself, "I forgive myself for what I did and I let myself go. That was then and this is now."

Whenever you think of something that you did in the past that you are still unhappy about, forgive yourself and let yourself go.

Recognize the Difference

One of the most important distinctions you can make is between a fact and a problem. What is the difference? A fact is something that is unchangeable. Your age is a fact. The size of the world is a fact. There are certain things that simply exist. They cannot be altered. They are facts.

One of the keys to happiness is for you never to become upset or angry about a fact. Just as you are not supposed to take out your anger on *things*, like kicking a piece of furniture, you shouldn't become angry or upset about facts. You simply accept them and get on with your life.

What, then, is a problem? A problem is something you can do something about. It can be solved. For example, a goal unachieved is merely a problem unsolved. You can focus your intelligence and ability on solving problems and achieving goals. Problems are simply things that you deal with as you go through life.

THE TIMES OF YOUR LIFE

As we said earlier, there are two time periods in your life, the past and the future. The present is a moment passing between the two. Into what category of time do we put facts, and into what category do we put problems?

The truth is that facts exist in the past. Something that happened in the past is a fact. It is unchangeable. This is important to understand because many people are miserable and unhappy in the present because something did not work out the way they expected it to sometime in the past. But because it happened, or didn't happen, in the past, it is an unchangeable fact. There is nothing you can do about it. Never become upset about a fact.

A problem exists in the future. This is something that you can do something about. This is a time period when you can channel your intelligence and ability into achieving a different result.

In anticipating the future and planning to achieve results, remember that the future has not happened yet and until it occurs nothing is certain. However, some people can anticipate and become attached to a future outcome, become anxious about that outcome, and then if it does not work out as planned they become afraid to take action in the future for fear that they may not succeed. Instead of thinking about the rewards of success, they become overwhelmed by the possibility of failure. This is the major reason for failure and underachievement in life.

THE THERAPEUTIC PROCESS

In psychotherapy, a lot of the work we do revolves around understanding the past and recognizing the normal and natural feelings of anger, depression, irritation, selfishness, arrogance, insecurity, and undeservingness that can be triggered by past events.

It is true that what has happened in the past is a fact and cannot be changed, but a big part of why people hang on to the past is because they have not grieved the loss of what could have or should have been. Feelings of regret and loss are triggered when people think about what might have been, and what they might have done differently. Often by delving deep into what the person expected to happen, and why she was disappointed, the psychotherapist and patient will arrive at a key assumption that is holding the person back. Once this false idea has been identified and understood, the individual's perspective will shift and her feelings will completely change.

BE YOUR OWN PSYCHOLOGIST

Think back to your past life and identify the worst possible thing that happened that could still be causing you to experience feelings of guilt, anger, or unworthiness. It takes tremendous ego strength to confront this negative experience, but almost everyone has had at least one big negative experience in their lives.

EXERCISE: When you think back and identify that one experience that continues to haunt you, ask yourself, "What were the circumstances? How did that situation occur in the first place?"

If you could go back and talk to the person you were in the past, what advice would you give to your younger self about the situation? What lesson did you learn through that experience that you might not have learned otherwise? Can you find something helpful or valuable that you gained from that experience?

Now, to be free of this past event, you must share it with at least one other person. It is in this willingness and ability to share this event, often what you still think of as an embarrassing or shameful experience, with one other trusted person that you become free from it forever.

Four Levels of Personality Development

There are four levels of mental and emotional development that each person needs to go through to be truly happy and free: *self-disclosure*, *self-awareness*, *self-acceptance*, and *self-esteem*.

1. SELF-DISCLOSURE

This is where you openly and honestly admit the mistakes you have made, the fears you have, the weaknesses you deal with, and the other hidden parts of your life that you are accustomed to keeping to yourself.

When you practice self-disclosure with at least one other

person whom you trust, you will find that it is not as bad as you may have thought for a long time. Self-disclosure can be a liberating experience.

2. SELF-AWARENESS

After self-disclosure, you can move on to the next level of personality development: *self-awareness*. When you practice self-disclosure and find surprisingly that the other person does not react in a negative or judgmental way, you become more aware of yourself.

Socrates taught that we learn something only by dialoguing about it with ourselves or others. The more you can talk out what you are thinking and feeling, the better you understand yourself and the situation. The more aware you become.

3. SELF-ACCEPTANCE

As you grow in self-awareness, you find that you are not a bad person, that you have many good qualities. You can then move to the next level of personal development: *self-acceptance*. You start to accept yourself as a good person. Your negative emotions of guilt and inferiority begin to fall away. You feel lighter and happier. Self-acceptance—seeing yourself "warts and all," as Oliver Cromwell said—is the stepping-stone to a healthy, happy personality.

4. SELF-ESTEEM REVISITED

Finally, you move to the highest level of personality development, that of self-esteem. Self-esteem is based on self-acceptance. The more you accept yourself and see yourself as a genuinely good person, the more you like and respect yourself. The more valuable and important you feel you are, the more you like others, and the more they like you.

As you move upward through the stages of self-disclosure, self-awareness, self-acceptance, and self-esteem, your life and your future open up to you like a summer sunrise. All the worries and negative feelings go away.

EXERCISE: Once you have gone through this process yourself, you can encourage your friends and family to go through the same process.

Expressing *unconditional positive regard* toward someone you care about—listening to him when he speaks, practicing nonjudgment no matter what he says—can be incredibly helpful. It can also be an amazing learning experience for you.

The Final Stage

The final stage of setting yourself free requires tremendous ego strength and self-confidence. This is when you gather up your courage and *apologize* to someone whom you have hurt in some way.

Because of the enormous power of justification, identification, rationalization, and hypersensitivity, the idea of apologizing to another person can be extremely stressful. But if you sincerely desire to be free from something you did in the past that you still feel bad about, you have no choice but to apologize.

In Alcoholics Anonymous, the 12-step program identifies a

crucial step toward personal growth and the healing process: *making amends* for any wrongdoing committed while in the grip of one's addiction. Taking responsibility for a previous mistake is not only a way to reconnect with someone you have wronged, but it also proves to yourself and to others that you are not the same person, and the person today acknowledges the effect of his or her previous behavior. Saying you are sorry allows you to let go and move forward.

Fortunately, this is a simple process. You can phone the other person right now and just say, "Hello, this is [your name] and I just wanted to call you and tell you that I am sorry for what happened, and I hope you will forgive me."

It doesn't matter how the other person responds. She may blow up and become angry. She may hang up. But surprisingly enough, the other person will often say, "I am so glad you called. I accept your apology. Why don't we get together for lunch in the near future?"

I have seen countless situations in which people who have been estranged for years have gotten back together and become good friends because one person had the strength of character just to say, "I'm sorry."

It may be even better for you to go and see the individual in person, if possible. At the very least, you can write a letter of apology and mail it.

Here is a key point with regard to apologizing: Resist the temptation to tell your side of the story, to defend yourself, or to justify your past behavior. When you attempt to explain or justify what you did to hurt the other person, it can be seen as "taking it back," leaving the situation unresolved. Just accept responsibility, say "I'm sorry," and leave it at that.

Finally, if you feel it is necessary and correct, offer to compensate or make restitution of some kind. Remember, in life you will make many mistakes, but you can never be too kind or too fair.

✦ ✦ ✦

CHAPTER FOUR

Change Your Thinking, Change Your Life

I have always believed, and I still believe, that whatever good or bad fortune may come our way, we can always give it meaning and transform it into something of value.

—HERMANN HESSE

It is not what happens to you in life that determines how you feel; it is how you respond to what happens.

Two people may have the same experience but one will rise above it, let it go, forget about it, and get on with his or her day or life. The other person will be crushed, angry, resentful, and often unhappy for an extended period of time. Same event, two different reactions.

A Course in Miracles says, "You give meaning to everything you see," and Shakespeare said, "Nothing is, but thinking makes it so."

The fastest way to transform from negative to positive, and to free yourself from the unhappy experiences of the past, is to resolve to see your past in a different way. When you practice the law of substitution and exchange a positive thought for a negative thought, your emotions change almost instantly.

Motivational speaker Wayne Dyer once said, "It's never too late to have a happy childhood."

Your Interpretation Style

In other words, by going back to your childhood and revising your memories of the unhappy experiences you had, you can turn them from bad to good, from depressing to elevating, and begin seeing your childhood in a totally new and positive way. By interpreting memories in a new way, you feel different about them.

In the Hindu religion, followers believe in multiple reincarnations. They believe that each person is born and dies over and over again for hundreds and thousands of years. At the end of each life, when you are reincarnated into another life, you move up to a higher level (toward salvation and oneness with the Supreme Soul), or down to a lower level (away from salvation), depending on how you behaved in your previous lifetime. Were you positive or negative, good or bad, helpful or hurtful?

The ultimate end of this process of reincarnation and progressive development, according to the Hindus, is the achievement of spiritual perfection on this earth. You then rise to *nirvana*, or heaven, and become free of the endless cycle of birth and death on this earth.

Whether or not you believe in reincarnation, here is an exercise you can do that can enable you to go back and have a happy childhood.

EXERCISE: Imagine that somewhere on the other side of the universe, long before you were born, you were able to search over the earth and select your next parents. In making this selection, you deliberately chose parents who would bring you into a situation in which you could learn the lessons that you most needed to learn in this next lifetime. You chose these parents so that you could experience the trials and tribulations of a life growing up in *this* family, because it was the only way you could learn, evolve, and grow into a better and finer person.

When you play with this idea, and look back at your parents, siblings, and childhood experiences, you will begin to identify the lessons you learned from each problem or difficulty you had while you were growing up. But now, by accepting that you chose your family yourself, you see them as valuable steps on your path of growth and development.

Think of the impact your parents have had on you. Can you identify how they have influenced your greatest strengths and weaknesses?

Learn from Those Experiences

Many people spend decades complaining about things that their parents did or did not do to or for them when they were growing up. That was true for me.

I remember once when I was in my early thirties and I was out on a date with a young woman. Over dinner, I started to recollect and complain about my father and how many mistakes he made with me during my childhood.

The young woman, quite intelligently, stopped me and asked, "Brian, are you happy to be alive?"

I said, "Of course! I really enjoy my life."

She then said, "Well, your father got you here, so stop complaining."

I remembered being momentarily stunned, and then I realized that she was right. From that day forward, I *never* complained about my father or my childhood again.

You can do the same. Whatever your parents did or didn't do, they got you here. They gave you the greatest gift of all—your life. You can always be grateful to them for that.

The Great Power That Loves You

Here is another exercise for you: Imagine that somewhere in the universe, there is a great power that loves you and wants the very best for you. This great power wants you to be happy, healthy, and fulfilled. It wants you to be successful and prosperous.

This great power also knows that you can rise to greater heights of happiness, joy, and pleasure only by learning certain essential lessons along the way. And it knows that you have a perverse nature; you will not learn unless it hurts.

You cannot learn from reading about or observing the experiences of others. You can learn only when you feel pain—physical, emotional, or financial. It takes pain to get your attention so that you can learn the lessons you are meant to learn.

Therefore, in order to teach you, train you, and guide you

toward your higher good, this great power sends you lessons, each accompanied by pain, so that you will listen and pay attention.

LOOK FOR THE GIFT

Norman Vincent Peale once said, "Whenever God wants to send you a gift, he wraps it up in a problem. The greater the gift that God wants to send you, the greater the problem he wraps it up in."

When you look into every problem or difficulty you have in your life as if it contained a gift of some kind, you begin to see things differently.

The challenge for most people is that they experience the pain but they are so busy complaining and blaming others that they don't see the gift.

YOUR BIGGEST PROBLEM

Think about all the problems that you have in your life right now.

Now imagine that this major problem has been sent to you containing a gift in the form of a lesson that you need to learn so that you can be happier and more successful in the future. What is that lesson?

One of the most powerful ways to change your thinking and your life is to seek the valuable lesson in every problem or difficulty you encounter. The most amazing thing is that if you look for a lesson in a setback or a difficulty, you will always find at least one lesson, and sometimes many.

EXERCISE: List three setbacks or temporary failures that you have experienced in your life. Now, can you reinterpret them and see them as learning experiences? What are the valuable lessons that the great power was trying to send you?

When you think about your biggest problem today, which usually involves another person, ask yourself, "What is the lesson I am meant to learn from this problem or difficulty?"

DIG DEEPER

Your first answer will usually be simple and superficial: "Maybe I should do more of this, or less of that."

But now comes the most important part. Ask yourself, "What *else* is the lesson that I am meant to learn in this situation?"

You drill down deeper. This time, the lesson will be more important and significant, if not painful. Perhaps you need to start doing something different, or stop something else altogether.

Then you ask again, "What *else* is the lesson that I am meant to learn?"

You drill even deeper. As you continue asking this question, the lessons will become more and more relevant and helpful, often more painful. Finally, if it is a major problem in your life that you have been wrestling with for a long time, you will reach the *real* lesson that you are meant to learn. It is usually that you need to change, get out of, or eliminate something in your current life.

FACE THE TRUTH

When you recognize the lesson contained in your unhappy situation and realize that you need to make a dramatic change in your life, you'll usually encounter ego problems. You avoid facing the situation. You practice denial, wishing and hoping that somehow it will get better on its own when in your heart, you know it never will.

When you finally develop the courage to face the truth about your situation and take the necessary actions dictated by that truth, something amazing will happen. All your stress will disappear. You will feel happy and at peace. You will feel calm and relaxed.

You've heard it said that denial is not a river in Egypt. Denial, or the refusal to face the truth or reality of your situation, is a major source of stress, anxiety, negative emotions, and even physical and mental illness.

The opposite of denial is acceptance. When you accept that the situation is the way it is, recognize that it is not going to change, and act accordingly, all your stress fades away.

Learned Optimism

Dr. Martin Seligman, of the University of Pennsylvania, one of the founders of positive psychology, conducted twenty-two years of research on the subject of optimism. One of his most important conclusions was that people are optimistic or pessimistic depending upon their *explanatory style*.

Your explanatory style is defined as "how you interpret events to yourself." Remember that perception is reality, and each person has his or her own perception of a situation. That's why they say there are always three sides to a story: the first person's, the second person's, and what actually happened.

In neurolinguistic programming, there are the concepts of *framing* and *reframing*. This is another way of describing explanatory style. It is not the situation that causes you to feel happy or unhappy. It is your *interpretation* of the situation to yourself as being either positive or negative. By reframing a past negative experience into a positive lesson, you will find that your emotional memory will totally shift and relieve you of those previous negative feelings.

CHOOSE YOUR WORDS CAREFULLY

Language is very important in this area. The words that you choose to use to interpret an event can trigger thoughts, feelings, emotions, and reactions, positive or negative. Words can make you happy or sad, encouraged or discouraged, excited or depressed.

One of the fastest ways to switch your mind from negative to positive when something goes wrong is to change your vocabulary. For example, instead of the word *problem*, use the word *situation*.

A problem is negative. It immediately conjures up images of loss, delay, and inconvenience. But the word *situation* is neutral. When you say, "We have an interesting situation here," there is no negative emotional charge attached to the word. As a result, you remain calm, clear, and more capable of dealing with whatever the situation might be.

SEE AN OBSTACLE AS A POSITIVE CHALLENGE

An even better word is *challenge*. Instead of reacting to a difficulty as if it were a problem, or a personal attack on you or your business, say, "We have an interesting challenge to deal with."

A challenge is something that you rise to. It brings out the best in you. It is positive and uplifting. We look forward eagerly to challenges that cause us to stretch and become even better by overcoming them.

The best word of all in describing a problem is *opportunity*. Instead of thinking about problems or difficulties, from now on, talk about the unexpected setbacks in your life as challenges or opportunities. An opportunity is something that we all want and look forward to eagerly. It is amazing how many of your greatest opportunities first appear as problems and difficulties.

Near-Death Experiences

Many people have experienced what is called a *near-death experience*. Usually in the midst of a surgery, they have actually died. Their hearts have stopped and their brainwave activity has seized. Fortunately, the miracles of modern medicine have resuscitated them and brought them back to life on the operating table.

Many of these people have reported a similar experience after having died. First of all, they saw themselves lying dead on the operating table with the doctors and nurses scrambling to bring their body back to life.

The second thing that these people report is a tremendous feeling of peace and relief. Nothing in their previous life seems important anymore. They are completely relaxed and experience a sense of bliss.

Third, they report seeing a distant bright light that they begin moving toward faster and faster. As they move toward this light, the feeling of peace, happiness, and even elation increases. They feel completely relaxed and at one with the universe as the light gets brighter and brighter.

THE LESSONS OF LIFE

The fourth common occurrence reported by people who have gone through a near-death experience is that on the "other side," they are asked two questions: "What have you learned in this lifetime?" and "How have you increased your capacity to love in this lifetime?"

Then, back on the operating table, the surgical staff resuscitates the body and brings it back to life. Suddenly, the person feels as though he or she is being sucked backward, away from the light, at an increasing speed. At a certain moment, everything goes black. The next thing people recall is waking up in a hospital room with members of their family and the medical staff around them.

So now we know. At the end of your life, there is a final exam. And we even know the questions on that exam. Throughout our lifetimes, one of our main goals is to develop excellent answers to those questions. This is the great business of life, to have these good answers. What have you learned, and how have you increased your capacity to love?

Reframe Your Experiences

When you reinterpret or reframe problems or difficulties, challenges or opportunities, you make a habit of looking for the good in every situation. When you look for something good in what initially appears to be a setback or difficulty, you will always find something positive. You will always find a benefit or an advantage. And the wonderful thing is that while you are looking for something good, your mind remains positive and optimistic. Your emotions remain calm and under control. It is impossible to experience stress and anxiety while you are looking for the good and seeking the valuable lesson.

A WORD FROM CHRISTINA

I once worked with a man who was suffering from complete disengagement at work and the inability to really enjoy anything in the rest of his life. He had a pessimistic view of the world and saw only the negative in every situation he experienced. Whenever something went wrong, he would personalize it and blame the problem on some weakness or characteristic within himself.

He assumed that the problem was direct proof that he wasn't smart enough, analytical enough, and so on. He walked around believing that anything that went wrong was because he was a bad person.

We had to work together reinterpreting and reframing his experiences in a positive way. He had to learn that sometimes things just happen, and that each experience provides an opportunity for growth. As he learned to shift his perspective from a pessimistic to an optimistic worldview at work, his ability to tolerate setbacks went way up. He bounced back from adversity faster. Overall he became a happier person by learning to interpret what happened to him in a positive way. And you can do the same.

Your job is to stay focused on the potential advantage or benefit of your current difficulties and keep your mind off the aspects of the situation that might make you angry or unhappy.

Problems and Crises

New Thought spiritual leader Emmet Fox wrote, "Great souls learn great lessons from small problems."

Your life will be an endless series of problems, difficulties, and challenges of all kinds. They come ceaselessly, like the waves of the ocean. They never stop; they only increase or decrease in intensity.

The only interruption to this endless series of problems will be the occasional crisis. If you are living an active life, you will probably have a crisis every two to three months. It may be a physical, financial, family, or personal crisis. But you will have a crisis of some kind.

By its very nature, a crisis comes unbidden. It is an unanticipated reversal or setback that you cannot prepare for or do anything about. The only real question, then, is whether you respond to it effectively or ineffectively.

If each person has a crisis of some kind every two or three months, it means that at this moment, you are in a crisis, or you have just gotten out of a crisis, or you are just about to have a crisis.

Your job is to take a deep breath when the crisis occurs, keep yourself calm, look for the good, seek the valuable lesson and then take action to reduce or minimize the crisis. We will talk about this at greater length in the next chapter.

Think About What You Want

The *law of concentration* says that whatever you dwell upon grows in your life.

The more you think about what you want and where you are going, the more positive and optimistic you remain. As Helen Keller said, "When you turn toward the sunshine, the shadows fall behind you."

In changing your thinking, you put a positive spin on those situations in your life that might make you feel unhappy for any reason. Look for the silver lining to the cloud. As Ralph Waldo Emerson said, "When the night is the darkest, the stars come out."

Many people suffer from worry and anxiety continually. Usually, this is learned from a parent who was also a worrier. Fortunately, most of the things that you worry about never happen. Instead, it is the things that you never thought to worry about that cause most of your unhappiness.

The Disaster Report

One of the best ways to stop worrying is to fill out a *Disaster Report* on every problem or difficulty that is causing you any worry or anxiety right now.

There are four steps to completing the Disaster Report:

Step 1: *Define* the worry situation clearly. What exactly are you worrying about?

Many people are worrying about something that is vague or unclear. Their thinking is confused. Like children in the night, they experience feelings of anxiety for reasons about which they are unclear. Or they do not have sufficient information, which can cause them to overreact. (Sometimes they are upset about something about which there is nothing they can do in any case.)

The very act of defining your worry situation clearly, in writing if possible, will often indicate an immediate solution that eliminates the worry situation completely. Doctors say that accurate diagnosis is half the cure.

Step 2: Determine the *worst possible outcome* of this worry situation. What is the worst thing that could possibly happen?

Most negative emotions and worry situations are caused by denial. The person feels under an enormous amount of stress because he is denying the reality of the situation. He does not want it to be true. He hopes that if he ignores it, it will go away. But this never works.

When you identify the worst thing that could possibly happen as a result of this worry situation, you often find that it is not as bad as you thought. It is something you can live with. It may be the end of a relationship, but it won't kill you. It may be the loss of a certain amount of money, but it won't bankrupt you. Even if it does bankrupt you, the worry situation is a *fact*, not a problem, and has to be faced. You'll earn the money back at a later time, doing something different in a different way and a different place.

If it is a health problem, resolve to confront it squarely. Refuse to play games with yourself. Do whatever you can to resolve the health problem, and then trust to the experts and to a higher power. There is a wonderful line from the Bible, Ephesians 6:13, ESV, that says, "Having done all, stand firm."

Step 3: Resolve to *accept the worst*, should it occur. Since most stress is caused by a refusal to identify the worst possible outcome and then a further refusal to accept it, once you resolve to accept the worst, your stress evaporates. You suddenly feel calm and at peace. When you replace denial with acceptance, you take full mental and emotional control of the situation.

Step 4: Begin immediately to *improve* upon the worst. Do everything that you possibly can to minimize the damage, control the costs, and cut your losses. Become so busy taking action to resolve your difficulties that you don't have any time left to worry.

Zero-Based Thinking

Finally, in changing your thinking and your life, practice *zero-based thinking* in every area of your life. Ask yourself, "Is there anything I am doing in my life that, knowing what I now know, I wouldn't do again if I had it to do over?"

It is amazing how much stress and unhappiness is caused by being in a situation that, knowing what you now know, you wouldn't get into again if you had it to do over.

It takes tremendous courage and character to admit that you made a mistake, that you changed your mind, and that you wouldn't get into this situation again if you had to do it over.

People hang on to the idea that once they've committed them-selves to something they must see it through at all costs. However, it is a strength, not a weakness, to admit you did not make the right decision, that you are not perfect. And you always have the right to change your mind with new information.

MOVE QUICKLY

Once you have determined that you would not get into that situation again, your next question is, "How do I get out, and how fast?"

It seems that as soon as you decide to take action to resolve a difficulty, your stress disappears. It is the uncertainty caused by in-action that generates most of the stress about the situation. The minute you decide to take action and resolve the situation, you feel a tremendous sense of relief and your course becomes clear.

You have an extraordinary mind. As the poet John Milton writes in *Paradise Lost*, "The mind is its own place, and in itself can make a heaven of hell and a hell of heaven."

Resolve today to use this wonderful mind of yours to think in a positive and constructive way about who you are, what you want, and where you are going.

From this moment on, refuse to interpret things to yourself in a negative way, a way that makes you unhappy, angry, and frus-trated. Instead, look for the good, and seek the valuable lesson. Approach each problem or difficulty as a challenge or oppor-tunity. Most of all, get so busy working on solving the problem and accomplishing the things that are important to you that you don't have time for worry or concern.

EXERCISE: Fill out the Disaster Report:

1. What is your biggest problem or worry right now?
2. What is the worst possible outcome of this situation?
3. If the worst-case scenario occurred, how would it affect you? Could you live with it? (Of course you could!)
4. Take action immediately to make sure that the worst does not happen—or if it has happened, get so busy solving the problem and minimizing the damage that you don't have any time to spare worrying about it. Do it now!

CHAPTER FIVE

✦ ✦ ✦

Become a Master of Change

*Events will take their course, it is no good our being angry at
them; he is happiest who wisely turns them to the best account.*

—EPICTETUS

The only thing constant in life today is change. Change is the law
of growth and growth is the law of life. It is amazing how many
people want things to get better but stay the same. This is simply
not possible.

Once upon a time, while Albert Einstein was teaching at
Princeton University, he had just administered an examination to
an advanced class of physics students and was on his way back to
his office. His teaching assistant was carrying the exams.

The teaching assistant had worked for Dr. Einstein for two
years. A bit hesitatingly, he asked, "Dr. Einstein, isn't this the
same exam that you gave to this same class last year?"

Einstein replied, "Yes, it is the same exam."

The teaching assistant was a bit confused. He asked, "Dr.

Einstein, how could you give the same exam to the same class two years in a row?"

Einstein replied simply, "The answers have changed."

In the fast-moving world of physics at that time, with new discoveries every few weeks, the same questions could actually generate different answers a year later.

YOUR ANSWERS ARE CHANGING

In your life, the same holds true. Your answers are changing at a more rapid rate than ever before. If someone were to ask you, "What was your biggest problem a year ago? What was your most important goal a year ago? What was your biggest challenge a year ago?" you would have a hard time remembering. The answers have changed completely.

EXERCISE: Identify the areas of your life where your answers are changing the most rapidly. What will you be doing one year from today based on the current direction of change?

Economists at Harvard University made three predictions some time ago. First, they said that in the next year, there will be more *change* in your industry than ever before. Second, there will be more *competition* in your industry than ever before. And third, there will be more *opportunities* in your industry than ever before, but they will be different from the opportunities of today. As it happens, these predictions were made in 1952, and have been true almost every year since then.

Thinking for a Change

What is the highest-paid work of all? The answer is thinking. Thinking is the highest-paid and most important work that you do, or that anyone else does. And this is for a specific reason.

The reason is consequences. In thirty years of studying time management and personal effectiveness, I have concluded that the *potential consequences* of doing or not doing something are the single most important consideration in terms of priorities.

An action is important if there are big potential consequences, positive or negative, of doing it or not doing it. An action is unimportant if it has low or no potential consequences. Your ability to correctly anticipate the likely consequences of an action is a hallmark of higher intelligence.

CONSIDER THE CONSEQUENCES

Of all the things you do, the quality of your thinking has the greatest consequences of all for your life. The quality of your thinking determines the quality of your decisions. The quality of your decisions determines the quality of your actions. The quality of your actions determines the quality of your results. And in life and work, results are everything.

Almost every great success in your life has been preceded by carefully thinking through what you are going to do and then doing it well and in a timely fashion. Almost every mistake in your life was the result of not thinking things through sufficiently. In both cases, the consequences of your thinking have a major impact on the quality of your life.

Your ability to think well determines how positive, happy,

and constructive you are. And it is determined by the "thinking tools" that you apply to a world of rapid change.

One of the greatest sources of stress, frustration, and unhappiness is an unwillingness or inability to deal with the inevitable impact of change in every area of your life. Fortunately, there are a series of tools that you can use to become a master of change rather than a victim of circumstances.

Expect It

We said earlier that most negative emotions arise from *frustrated expectations*. You expect something to happen in a certain way, and when it doesn't, you become angry and often lash out at others as the cause of your disappointment. But when you use your superior thinking abilities, you will begin to expect change as a normal, natural, and inevitable part of life. Like a willow tree, you will bend with the winds of change, rather than snapping like a pine tree when the storms of life come through.

There are three factors driving change in the world of business and careers today: information explosion, technology expansion, and competition.

INFORMATION EXPLOSION

The amount of information in any field is doubling every two to three years, and in some technical fields, much faster. More than five million books and articles are published each year, in magazines, newspapers, and newsletters of all kinds. And one small piece of data amid this information avalanche can have a major impact on your life, your work, and your family.

In Disney's animated version of *Alice in Wonderland*, the White

Rabbit is always running anxiously in place, saying, "I'm late, I'm late, for a very important date!"

Later, in the sequel, *Through the Looking Glass*, the Queen says to Alice, "Now, here, you see, it takes all the running you can do, to keep in the same place. If you want to get somewhere else, you must run at least twice as fast as that!"

Today, just to stay even with your field, and to maintain your current income, you must be continually reading in your field, learning new ideas and ways of doing your job better. It's hard not to feel like the White Rabbit, frantically running around the Queen's country to stay afloat, let alone move forward!

TECHNOLOGICAL EXPANSION AND CHANGE

The second factor driving change today is technology. Hundreds of thousands, perhaps millions, of the finest minds that have ever lived are working day and night to develop technology that does things faster, better, cheaper, and more conveniently than anything that currently exists. The rule is that if it is on the market, it is already obsolete.

Just to stay even, you must continually master new technologies, learning how to use and apply them to improve your life and get your job done faster. Look at what has happened in our lives with the introduction of the iPhone and all the apps and capabilities it makes available to us. What will be invented in the future is almost beyond our imagination.

COMPETITION

The third factor driving change is the growth of competition. Millions of people all over the world are driven and determined to improve the quality of their lives by producing and selling products and services of a higher quality and at a lower price to customers everywhere—and, thus, increasing the success of their businesses. To survive and thrive in our modern market society, you must be as determined and aggressive as your competitors in serving your customers. You have to run twice as hard just to stay in the same place.

Customers today are more demanding, disloyal, and self-centered than ever before. They have more choices and more knowledge about what they want and what they have to pay to get it. They are fickle, willing to drop a longtime supplier immediately for a better combination of price and quality somewhere else. Look at what Jeff Bezos of Amazon has accomplished by offering millions of products at reduced prices with overnight delivery. As of 2017, he was the third-richest man in the world because of his ability to serve customers faster.

You can be sure of only one thing. Whatever you are doing today, you have to be doing it vastly better one year from now just to keep your job. You must be continually upgrading your skills and your ability to get more and better results. Like a runner in a race, if you slow down, the other runners will pass you and you may find it impossible to catch up.

Change in Your Personal Life

You should also expect changes in your marriage and in your relationships with other people. As people grow and mature, they develop new tastes, more definite personalities, and different goals and aspirations, and they often become completely different people.

You have heard of the seven-year itch. It seems there is a cycle of seven years in almost every part of human life. Over the course of seven years, people, children, spouses, companies, jobs, and your own wants and desires evolve and change, sometimes completely.

Every cell in your body is brand-new every seven years. Every cell of your skin is brand-new every thirty days. As you grow and mature, your level of fitness, overall health, bodily image, and levels of energy will continue to change, sometimes in ways that you may not like.

The Passages of Life

In the book *Passages*, Gail Sheehy writes that adults go through major transitions approximately every ten years. Between the ages of 18 and 22, people go from dependent teenagers to largely self-sufficient adults. Between the ages of 28 and 32, they go from a time of experimentation to one of settling down into marriages and careers. From 38 to 42, people settle into their careers and families, largely stabilize their lives, and begin to realize that many of the things they originally planned to do with their lives are not going to happen. Between the ages of 48 and 52, people get settled more deeply into their careers, often divorce and go their separate ways, and begin thinking about the second half of life and retirement. And finally, from 58 to 62, most people are quite resigned to their lives and to what they have accomplished or failed to accomplish. They are more concerned with comfort, security, and retirement as they look toward their seventies and eighties.

Changes Are Inevitable

The point is that at each stage of your life, you are going to go through major changes and transitions. Don't be surprised, shocked, or disappointed. Instead, expect these changes as inevitable. This dramatically lowers your stress levels and increases your ability to navigate these changes in a positive and constructive way. As business and management visionary Peter Drucker wrote, "The very best way to predict the future is to create it."

There is an essential skill, called *mental preparation*, you can learn that will enable you to master change throughout your life. In mental preparation, you relax and visualize yourself experiencing changes sometime in the future. In your mind's eye, you see yourself responding to these changes in a calm, positive, and constructive way. Instead of reacting or overreacting when things don't work out the way you expect, you accept the inevitable changes as a normal and natural part of adult life.

By acknowledging and preparing yourself for change, knowing that it is inevitable, you can savor each precious moment with the knowledge that it soon will evolve into something else. By pausing and taking in a special moment or happy time in your life, you both acknowledge that it will change and prepare to let go of it. When you do this, you will move easily through life's changes rather than getting stuck and resisting the inevitable.

Anticipate It

One of the most powerful thinking tools you can develop is called *extrapolatory thinking*. This requires that you look down the road of life and think about all the things that could possibly happen.

Practice *crisis anticipation*. Make a list of the worst things that could happen in your personal and business lives. Think about possible death, injury, financial reversals, bankruptcy, and unexpected events that could derail your most cherished hopes, dreams, and plans.

In thinking ahead and identifying the worst things that could happen, imagine what you could do to deal with those events should they occur. What steps could you take today to guard against those negative events? Of all the things you could do, what should you do first?

Some large companies practice what is called *scenario planning*. They look at every aspect of their business and imagine the different things that could happen nationally and internationally that could disrupt their business in any way. They then develop scenarios, or complete plans of action, to deal with those negative events if they were to occur.

By practicing extrapolatory thinking, crisis anticipation, and scenario planning, you can dramatically lower your stress levels and increase your effectiveness by anticipating the many things that could happen and then creating plans to deal with them.

Develop Long-Term Perspective

The late political scientist Dr. Edward Banfield, of Harvard University, determined through fifty years of research that the most successful people in our society had what he called *long-term perspective*. They made a habit of looking far into the future, ten or twenty years out, and imagining what could possibly happen at that time. They then determined what steps they could take in the present to assure that their long-term goals came true, and that the negative things that could happen did not occur.

One of the major causes of stress, anxiety, and worry has to do with money. Many people are undisciplined regarding their money and, as a result, they spend it all each month, and a little more besides. Millions of people end up declaring personal bankruptcy every year because of a failure to think ahead financially.

Plan Your Financial Affairs

One of the actions you can take to improve the quality of your life is to plan every aspect of your financial affairs in detail. Develop a plan for financial accumulation and follow it. Spend less than you earn, and save or invest the balance. Build up cash reserves so that you are prepared for any sudden reversal.

As a business owner or executive, make a habit of thinking long term. Look into the future of your business and anticipate the changes and trends that could affect your sales and profitability. Rather than allowing yourself to be surprised by change, anticipate it and take action accordingly.

Jack Welch, former CEO of General Electric, once said, "The reality principle is the most important principle of leadership. . . . Reality means that you see the world as it really is, not as you wish it were."

What skills, talents, and abilities will you personally—and your company—require to lead your industry in the years ahead? What products, services, and capabilities will you and your company need to continue to grow in sales and profitability? What customers will you be serving in the future, and what will they be demanding from you that is different from today?

Especially, who will your competition be in the future, and what is your plan to succeed against them?

Develop More Options

One of the great rules for success is: You are only as free as your well-developed options.

The more options you have, the greater freedom you have. The more options you develop, by upgrading your skills, broadening your product or service lines, and anticipating the worst things that could happen, the greater control you have over your personal and business destiny.

Remember, hope is not an option. Wishing is not an option. Expecting that everything will work out for the best is not an option either. Only a clearly written, thought-through plan of action gives you the kind of options you need to anticipate change and then to master it on a regular basis.

Look Ahead

If your business collapsed, your job disappeared, your income vanished, and all your assets were gone, what would you do then? Because of unexpected changes in information, technology, and competition, these setbacks happen to large numbers of people every year. The ones who survive and thrive are those who anticipate these possibilities and make provision against them.

Assume that you will be in a completely new field, in a new career, in a new industry, doing a new job, in five years. What new skills, knowledge, and abilities will you need at that time to be able to provide for yourself and assure a high standard of living?

It is amazing how many people are unhappy, frustrated, and stuck because they never took the time to sit down and anticipate the inevitable changes that will sweep over them in the future. Don't let this happen to you.

Prepare for It

The mark of the superior person and the true professional in any field is preparation. Top people do their homework and are thoroughly prepared for whatever might happen.

The time to take a first-aid course is well before the accident. The time to develop a new skill is before you need it. It is too late to begin thinking about preparing or developing a new skill after you have been bowled over by the unexpected wave of change.

One of the qualities of top people is that they practice *future orientation* most of the time. Future orientation is the mark of leaders and the top thinkers in our society. They think well ahead, down the road of life, and imagine what they will have to do to prepare for that future.

Imagine a Magic Wand

Practice the "magic wand" exercise. As you think into the future, imagine that you could wave a magic wand and make your life perfect in the following four critical areas that determine most of your happiness or unhappiness.

EXERCISE: Take out a notebook and answer the following questions. Pay attention to your internal dialogue and apply the concepts you've learned from earlier chapters.

1. If your job, business, and income were ideal in five years, what would they look like? How would they be different from today?

2. If your family, relationships, home, and lifestyle were perfect in five years, what would they look like? And how would they be different from today?

3. If your level of health and fitness were perfect in five years, how would you look and feel? How much would you weigh? How much would you exercise each day? What foods would you eat? And especially, how would you be different from today?

4. Finally, if your financial situation were perfect in five years, how much would you have in the bank, and how much passive income would you be earning each month and each year?

Practice Idealization

One of the most important behaviors of top people is *idealization*. In idealizing, you create a vision of a perfect future for yourself in every area of your life. You practice no-limit thinking. You imagine that you have all the time and money, all the friends and contacts, all the education and experience, and all the talents and abilities that you could possibly need in order to be, have, or do anything. If this were your situation, what would you really want to do with your life?

When you combine idealization with the magic wand exercise, you liberate your mind from the constraints of day-to-day work and bill paying. You practice what is called *blue-sky thinking*, a hallmark of top people and peak performers in every area. You imagine that you have the whole blue sky above you and no limits except for your own imagination.

A WORD FROM CHRISTINA

Often when I spend time with my husband and we are trying to decide what to do with our day, I ask him, "Honey, if this were your perfect day, what would you do with it?" I then tell him what my perfect day would look like, and we find a way to combine the elements of each of our two perfect days.

What do you have to do, starting today, to begin creating the ideal future that you desire? Peter Drucker said, "People vastly *overestimate* what they can do in one year, but they vastly underestimate what they can do in five years."

Plan for Your Future

There is a *six P formula* for success in life: Proper prior planning prevents poor performance." There are no guarantees in life, but you can dramatically increase the likelihood that you will create a wonderful life for yourself by deciding what that wonderful life would look like and then preparing every detail thoroughly in advance.

One of the most important parts of preparation has to do with your level of knowledge and skill. Perhaps the greatest time-saver of all is to get better at the most important things you do. The better you get at your key tasks, the greater will be the results and rewards you achieve, in less time. As a result, you will get paid more and promoted faster than in any other way.

Earlier we talked about the importance of accepting responsibility for every part of your life. There is perhaps no area that is more important than your accepting responsibility for preparing yourself for the kind of future that you desire. Don't trust to luck. Things work out well only for people who make them work out well, because they prepare thoroughly in advance.

Whatever changes you are likely to experience in the months and years ahead, the more thoroughly you prepare, the calmer and more effective you will be. Your stress levels will be greatly reduced and your levels of optimism and happiness will be greatly increased.

A WORD FROM CHRISTINA

As a mother and a professional I know that the difference between having a smooth, effective day and a chaotic, stressful one comes down to planning the day and organizing accordingly. At the beginning of the week I sit down *for an hour and plan out the whole week in my planner (my favorite is Planner Pad). There is something calming and organizing about writing things down. I check every day and add new items if necessary. This keeps me grounded and far more effective with my time than if I hadn't planned out the week in advance. I've encouraged my friends and clients to practice this simple activity and they all tell me what an amazing difference it makes. It gives them a tremendous sense of control.*

Analyze It

Many negative emotions are triggered by an inappropriate over-reaction to an unexpected setback or difficulty. It is vital that you carefully analyze a problem when it occurs to assure that you thoroughly understand it and to determine what you can do to deal with it or resolve it.

Elisabeth Kübler-Ross, the psychiatrist who specialized in helping people deal with a death in the family, outlined several stages that people go through upon learning about the death of someone who was close to them. She found that people have to progress through these natural stages to reach the other side, where they can be at peace and get on with the rest of their lives.

When you deal with major life disruptions, you go through these same stages. The only question is how quickly you get through them and get back to normal.

The more thoughtfully you analyze the changes that are

taking place, the faster you master them and take control of your emotions and your behavior.

SIX STAGES OF GRIEF

(Note: Kübler-Ross's theory covers the first five stages; we added the sixth.)

Stage 1: Denial—The first reaction to a sudden reversal or traumatic experience is to think, "This can't be happening!" or "This cannot have happened!" Even when faced with the reality of the event, many people immerse themselves in denial long after it is clear that the negative situation has occurred. You see this continually with major business reversals and career or marriage setbacks.

Stage 2: Anger—The natural tendency of most people is to lash out and blame someone else, or themselves, when something negative and unexpected happens. They justify, rationalize, and try to convince themselves that this shouldn't have happened and someone is to blame.

Stage 3: Bargaining—The individual negotiates with herself and others to minimize her role or responsibility in the event, or to diminish the severity of what has happened.

Stage 4: Depression—At this point, the individual realizes that the situation has occurred, and it cannot be changed. The person has died, the money is lost, the career or marriage has ended, and there is nothing that she can do about it. She feels helpless, passive, and very much like a victim.

Stage 5: Acceptance—Finally, the individual gets control of herself and her emotions and accepts that what has happened is unchangeable and is now a fact that can't be altered. She pulls herself together and begins thinking about the future.

Stage 6: Resurgence—The individual gets up, gets going, and gets busy, taking action to deal with the new reality. She takes control of her life and emotions, feels positive and optimistic, and begins moving ahead.

The most important question regarding any major setback or disappointment in life is: How long does it take you to move completely through the negative experience, from denial to resurgence? Some people take days or weeks; some take months or years. Some people never recover.

The Power of Asking Questions

One of the ways that you can take control of a negative situation is by analyzing it carefully. You do this by asking the following questions. It is not possible to remain upset, angry, and out of control while you are asking questions and seeking to understand the change that has taken place.

"What exactly has happened?" At this stage, strive for accuracy. Refuse to attack or blame someone or something else for what has occurred. Focus on clarity and understanding.

"How did it happen?" Imagine that you are gathering evidence

for a third party; you are more concerned with accuracy than with recrimination. Ask follow-up questions so that you thoroughly understand the details.

"What can be done?" Take control of your thinking by focusing on the future—on what can be done—rather than what has happened, which cannot be changed. This makes you more positive and puts you in control of the situation.

"What actions do I take now?" Instead of worrying or wallowing in self-pity or remorse, get busy taking whatever actions you can to resolve the situation and move forward.

EXERCISE: Think of a recent setback or negative experience you have had and apply these four questions. Notice how going through the process of asking and answering these questions changes your experience of the situation.

Seek First to Understand

Stephen R. Covey, bestselling author of *The 7 Habits of Highly Effective People*, said, "Seek first to understand, then to be understood." Focus on asking questions to keep yourself calm and your mind clear.

Avoid the tendency to catastrophize, thinking or assuming the very worst in a difficult situation. Most situations are not as bad as they first appear, and very often what has happened cannot be changed in any case.

Avoid the natural inclination to confuse correlation with causation. One of the biggest thinking mistakes that people make is jumping to conclusions. When two events happen at the same time, many people immediately assume that one event caused the other. In most cases, however, the two events happening together are merely a coincidence. Neither of the events has anything to do with the other.

The key to analyzing a situation, to keeping yourself calm and in control, is to continue to ask questions and gather information. Sometimes, what appeared to be a major setback or problem turns out not to be as serious as you thought. It may even be an opportunity.

Take Advantage of It

When you experience a major reversal in life, immediately change your language from *problem* and instead use the word *situation*, *challenge*, or *opportunity*.

Many of the best experiences of your life will initially appear as a setback or difficulty. Your job is to turn it to your advantage if you can.

W. Clement Stone, a self-made multimillionaire, was famous for responding to every problem with, "That's good!" He would then encourage everyone to look into the situation to find something good about it. And they always did.

Look for the good in every difficulty you face in your life. Continually imagine that each contains a benefit or advantage that you can use.

Seek the valuable lesson. Imagine that the universe is trying to teach you a lesson that will help you to be happier and more successful in the future. What could it be?

Self-Made Millionaires

The average self-made millionaire in America has been broke or nearly broke 2.3 times before finally becoming wealthy. But the reason that these people became millionaires was because of the lessons they learned from their earlier mistakes. If they had not failed in business at an earlier age, they would never have developed the knowledge and wisdom necessary to succeed later. The bankruptcy or business failure was traumatic at the time, but it contained the seeds of future wealth.

Finding the Ideal Person

Many people go through a bad marriage or relationship. It ends with anger, bitterness, and negative feelings. Later on, that same person meets the ideal mate, settles down, and is happy for the rest of his or her life.

In retrospect, many happily married people look back at a negative relationship as having been essential for them to recognize the right relationship when it came along. They realized that if they had stayed in that bad relationship, they would have been miserable for months or even years. It seems that, as I've said before on many occasions, "problems come not to obstruct, but to instruct."

How People Learn

As it happens, humans learn only from suffering. They learn only from pain. This is inevitable. But what is really dumb is if people experience the pain but then fail to identify the lesson that goes with it. This just makes it far more likely that they will make the same mistake again.

This especially applies to people and the way they treat their health. Often people won't invest much time and effort in taking care of themselves until they are diagnosed with an illness or suffer from chronic pain.

Neutralize the Negative Emotion

Since change is inevitable, whenever you have a reversal of any kind, you can neutralize your feelings toward it by saying, "I see the angel of God in every change."

Look upon change as a blessing containing ideas, insights, and advantages that you can use to go on to create an even more wonderful life in the future.

Resistance of any kind is a major source of stress, negativity, and even depression. The opposite of resistance is acceptance that a change has taken place in your life, and then moving on. It is said that whatever you resist persists.

Practice Acceptance

One of the great rules for success is to accept things that have happened and that you cannot change. Accepting a fact as a reality is the first step to taking charge of yourself and your emotions, and then moving on to something higher and better.

The inability to get over a bad experience is a major block that holds people back, often for many years. One of the marks of superiority is accepting that you are not perfect, that you make mistakes, and that you have made bad choices and decisions in the past, which have led to bad results and consequences. Mistakes are what make us human.

Have No Regrets

A psychiatrist with twenty-five years of experience once said that the most common words he ever heard at the beginning of a period of emotional counseling were "If only . . ."

People told stories of their suffering, tragedies, and reasons for their unhappiness, beginning with the words "If only . . ." They said, "If only I had not taken that action, made that decision, accepted that job, invested in that company, or married that person."

It is sad how often regret over mistakes we have made in the past hold us back from taking advantage of the opportunities of the future.

One of the great secrets of success is to eliminate the phrase "if only" from your vocabulary. Never say those words again. Accept that whatever happened happened. Perhaps in retrospect it was unfortunate, but in any case, it is over and done with. It is a part of the past. It is a fact. It cannot be changed.

Stop thinking that you are special or chosen in some way, or that undesirable changes are not going to take place in your life and work. When they do occur, accept responsibility, focus on the future, and get busy solving your problems and achieving your goals.

The Great Discovery

You become what you think about most of the time.

Most of the time, successful, happy people think about what

they want and how to get it. Unsuccessful, unhappy people think about what they don't want, especially things that occurred in the past and who is to blame for their problems.

William James said, "The first step in dealing with any problem in life is to be *willing* to have it so."

Tell yourself, "What cannot be cured must be endured." Remind yourself that you are not a victim. You are a proud, confident, self-reliant person in complete charge of your life and your future. Refuse to wallow in regret or remorse about things and changes that have happened that you cannot control or have any effect on.

Fear of Loss

The first major motivation in life is the desire for gain. The second major motivation is the fear of loss. As it happens, people fear loss two and a half times more intensely than they desire gain. They may be motivated to a certain degree to achieve gain, but they are absolutely devastated when they suffer a loss, or even *think* about losing something.

If you have ever had a happy relationship, a good job, or a stable financial situation and you have lost it for any reason, you can find yourself immersed in grief and regret, often for many months or years. To bounce back from a reversal, it is important to remind yourself that you were OK *before* you had the job or relationship and you will be OK again in the future without it.

The solution is to accept the reality of the situation, whatever it is. Refuse to resist or fight against it. Stop feeling sorry for yourself and telling yourself that *if only* you had done something different, this unfortunate event would not have happened.

Sunk Costs

In accounting, there are a series of costs that are taken into consideration on the balance sheet. One of them is called a *sunk cost*, defined as an amount of money that has been spent and that now is gone forever. In a business, this can include advertising that does not induce customers to buy a product, producing goods that do not sell, or any expenditure from which there is no future benefit. The money is gone.

Very often in life you have sunk costs as well. You can invest enormous sums of time, money, and emotion in people, jobs, and investments. But unexpected setbacks and difficulties occur and your investment turns out to have been wasted.

Instead of throwing good money after bad, investing more time and emotion in a bad relationship, or spending more time on something that obviously has no chance of success, you must accept that it is a sunk cost and resolve to let it go.

When you develop the strength of character to say things like, "I was wrong; I made a mistake; I've changed my mind," you find that it is much easier to let go of unfortunate events that have occurred and simply accept them as a normal and natural part of your personal growth and development.

Take Responsibility for It

Perhaps the greatest source of personal power is to deal with the change by accepting 100 percent responsibility for everything that has happened. This allows you to take control of yourself and your emotions, and often the situation itself.

A major cause of the negative emotions that hold you back is the anger, fear, resentment, envy, and jealousy that accompany an unhappy experience. Each of these emotions depends for its existence on blaming either yourself or someone else.

As you know by now, when you stop blaming others and accept complete responsibility, all your negative emotions stop, as if shut off like a light.

Think About the Solution

One of the ways to take responsibility for a change or problem in your life is to become intensely solution oriented.

When most people experience reversals and failures, they immediately lash out and look for someone to blame, someone who is at fault. Instead, you resolve, from this day forward, to focus on the solution rather than the problem.

First of all, refuse to make excuses. A fully functioning person is non-defensive. If he has made a mistake, he admits it, and focuses all his energy on minimizing or resolving the mistake.

Refuse to criticize anybody for anything. Criticism is something that a child learns by being criticized from a young age. Many children grow up to be extremely critical of others, for whatever they do or fail to do. Criticizing others is actually a sign of weakness on your part. It wastes your time and stops you from dealing with the situation and finding a solution.

Refuse to complain about your situation, or about anything else. As Henry Ford II once said, "Never complain, never explain." If you are not happy about the situation, do something to resolve it. If you cannot change it, resolve to accept it. But never complain.

When you criticize or complain, it makes you weak and

ineffective. You position yourself as a victim, a passive person who has little or no control of yourself or your life. People who criticize and complain are always negative and unhappy. They have ongoing feelings of inferiority and unworthiness. They get into a downward spiral that makes them weak and unpleasant people.

Think About Next Time

One of the keys to taking responsibility for any situation is to use the phrase "Next time." Focus on the future rather than the past. When you have a difficulty or problem, say, "Next time this occurs, why don't we . . ."

You can say, "In the future, I will . . ."

Especially if you are a parent or a boss, and your children or staff drop the ball and disappoint you, remember that you are the person in charge. You must step up, accept responsibility, and focus on the solution rather than the problem.

Keep saying to yourself: "I am responsible!"

As soon as you accept responsibility for a problem or situation, your mind becomes calm and clear, and you take complete control. You think with greater clarity, act with greater confidence, and make better decisions. By accepting responsibility for unexpected changes and difficulties, you become a leader in your family, your organization, and your life.

Adapt and Adjust to It

Charles Darwin wrote, "Survival goes not necessarily to the strongest or the most intelligent of the species, but to the one most adaptable to change." Your ability to recognize, accept, anticipate, and adapt to change is the mark of a superior mind and a positive personality. The more rapidly you recognize that a change has taken place and is now irrevocable, the faster you can begin adjusting to the change and taking advantage of it.

Because of the accelerating rate of change in information, technology, and competition, each of them building and magnifying the effects of the others, you must be continually calling a time-out to address the new realities of the current situation.

Each time a change takes place in your life or work, and especially when you experience resistance or frustration trying to do things the same old way, take time to rethink your situation. Mentally cut yourself free from the past. Think about who you are and what you want within the context of the new circumstances.

Reevaluate your situation to be sure that what you are doing is still consistent with your long-term goals and ambitions. Sometimes when you experience setbacks, difficulties, and resistance, it is an indication that you are on the wrong track, that you are attempting to do something that may not be the best choice for you.

Avoid the Comfort Zone

Sir Isaac Newton's First Law of Motion states, in part, that a body at rest will remain at rest unless acted on by an unbalanced force.

This is the *law of inertia*. In personal life, it explains the principle of the comfort zone. People become comfortable in a particular situation, even if it is not working out or is not the best for them. They then resist any information or feedback that suggests that perhaps they are on the wrong track.

When you take the time to reevaluate your situation based on the current reality, you often see the necessity of doing something different. You must always remain open to the necessity of change.

Be prepared to reorganize your life as well. The natural tendency of most people is to get into fixed routines and do things the same way, over and over again, until it becomes a habit. People establish rituals in their personal and business lives that they follow unthinkingly, even if these rituals or habits are no longer the best ways of living or dealing with a particular relationship or situation.

EXERCISE: What areas of your life could you reorganize to help your life to flow more smoothly and more in harmony with what you really want? What should you be doing more of, or less of? What should you start doing, or stop doing altogether?

Restructure Your Life

Be prepared to restructure your life in each area, especially with regard to your family and your work. In restructuring, you apply the *80/20 rule*, which says that 80 percent of your results comes from 20 percent of your activities. When you restructure your life, you focus more time and attention on the 20 percent of things you do that give you the very best results in terms of financial success and personal satisfaction.

When you look at your business life, you will find that 20 percent of your activities accounts for 80 percent of your results, and 80 percent of your hopes and dreams for promotion and higher pay. At home, you'll discover that 20 percent of the things you do gives you 80 percent of your happiness and satisfaction in your personal life and with your family. In restructuring, you focus more and more of your time on those activities that give you the greatest personal and career payoffs.

Look for ways to continually reengineer your life and work. *Reengineering* is another word for *simplification*. When you practice reengineering in your life, you look for ways to do things more simply and easily. Sometimes you can reengineer your life by reducing or even eliminating activities that have become habits but that no longer contribute as much to your life or work as other activities could.

You can delegate low- or no-value tasks to others, thereby freeing up your time to do more of the things that give you the greatest results and satisfaction. You can outsource tasks such as housecleaning, lawn maintenance, laundry, and even meal preparation to people who specialize in those areas and who can often do them faster, more easily, better, and more cheaply than you can.

Whenever you feel overwhelmed with too much to do and too little time, which can cause you tremendous amounts of stress, stand back and look at your life, and think about how you could reengineer and simplify it in every area.

Reinvent Your Life

Practice reinvention on a regular basis. You reinvent your life when you imagine yourself starting over today in light of the current situation. For example, imagine that your job or industry disappeared overnight and you had to begin a new job or career.

EXERCISE: Imagine that you had no limitations. If you were starting over, what job would you want to do? Where would you want to work? How much would you want to earn?

If you could do anything at all, what would you choose to do? If you were financially independent, how would you change your current life? You should think about reinventing yourself every six to twelve months throughout your life in order to respond effectively to the unstoppable rate of change.

Regain Control

You regain control when you rethink, reevaluate, reorganize, restructure, reengineer, and reinvent your life. You free yourself from the baggage of the past and instead concentrate on the possibilities of the future. You feel a tremendous sense of personal power and confidence. You put yourself in charge of your life, rather than allowing your life to be determined by the decisions of the past or the pressures of the present.

Finally, you engage in *resurgence*. This is when you counterattack the frustrations and stresses in your life. You take action boldly in the direction of your dreams and goals. You sit in the driver's seat of your own life, put your hands on the wheel, and decide your own direction.

Become Action Oriented

The natural tendency of most people, when they are faced with rapid change or unexpected reversals, is to feel stunned, and to become passive. They feel frustrated and unable to move. They stop and wait, hoping and expecting that someone or something else will come along to get them unstuck.

But all successful people are intensely *action oriented*. They think in terms of what they can do rather than waiting for someone else to come along and take care of them or the situation. They develop a sense of urgency, and a bias for action. They keep moving forward. And in moving forward, just as in skiing, the faster you move, the greater control you have.

Respond to It

As previously mentioned, your life will be a continuous series of problems and crises. By their very nature, crises come unbidden and unexpected. The only part of a crisis that you can control is your response to it. Do you stand up to your problems and take positive action or do you let them overwhelm you?

Nobel Prize–winning author and historian Arnold Toynbee studied the rise and fall of civilizations through the ages. Based on his work, he developed the *challenge-and-response* theory of history.

He found that each civilization began as a small tribe or group of people that was faced with a challenge or a confrontation that threatened its very survival. In response, the group reorganized itself to confront and deal with the challenge effectively. As a result, it survived and grew larger.

But each growth triggered even greater challenges from external forces, usually hostile tribes or armies. With each step forward, the group would be faced with an even greater challenge, to which it would have to respond effectively to continue to survive and thrive.

CHALLENGE-AND-RESPONSE

The twenty-seven great civilizations of history each began with a single tribe. In the case of the Mongols, who built the largest empire in world history, it began with three people.

What Toynbee concluded was that a civilization would continue to grow as long as it responded effectively to the inevitable challenges that it faced in the process of growth, especially in competition with other civilizations, nations, and tribes.

In your life, it is the same. Every challenge you face requires that you respond, either effectively or ineffectively. When you respond effectively, you grow as a person in knowledge, wisdom, and skill. This new growth inevitably triggers another challenge of some kind, to which you must also respond effectively. This process goes on and on throughout your life.

The only part of the challenge-and-response theory that you can control is your response to the inevitable ups and downs of life. By resolving in advance that you will respond effectively, you mentally prepare yourself to deal with anything the world throws at you. As Nietzsche wrote, "That which does not kill us, makes us stronger."

Your level of "response-ability" in the face of the inevitable challenges of personal and business lives is the true measure of your character and skill. Leaders are those who respond effectively, over and over again, and as a result are given ever greater challenges to respond to.

Look upon everything that happens to you as a challenge, something that you can rise to and in so doing, become better and stronger as a person. The better and stronger you become, the happier and more successful you will be in every area of your life.

Embrace Change as Progress

From this day forward, welcome change as the key to progress. It is not possible to grow, mature, and realize everything you are capable of without a continual amount of turbulence and disruption in your life.

Change your vocabulary. Replace the word *change* with the word *improvement*.

Every change contains within it an opportunity for you to improve the quality of your life and work. Is the glass half-full or half-empty? The optimist is always looking for the good, and how she can benefit from a change in conditions, rather than feeling sorry for herself and lashing out at those she feels are responsible.

As an exercise, assume that you are being guided by a great power and that all change in your life is aimed at helping you to be happier and more successful in the future. This attitude makes you a more positive person.

In our seminars, we tell people that when they set a big, new goal for themselves, their lives will often go into a period of disruption. Someone may set a goal to double his income and suddenly find himself laid off or fired the following week. Later he finds a new job, and in that job, he gets an opportunity to earn twice as much as ever before. In retrospect, he realizes that if he had not been fired, he would have stayed, by the law of inertia, in the old job indefinitely. He concludes that getting fired is

God's way of telling him that he was in the wrong job in the first place.

When a relationship does not work out, imagine that it is part of a great plan to make you happier and more successful in the future. Losing a relationship or marriage is probably God's way of telling you that you were in the wrong situation to start with. Instead of becoming angry and frustrated and blaming other people for the change, assume that it is all part of a great plan to move you upward and onward to the fulfillment of your potential.

Many of our greatest changes and disruptions in life do not look like something good when we first experience them. But as you adapt, adjust, and respond effectively to the change, it can often be exactly what you need to become more and more of what you are truly capable of becoming.

✦ ✦ ✦

CHAPTER SIX

The People in Your Life

You will find as you look back upon your life that the moments that stand out, the moments that you have really lived, are the moments that you have done things in a spirit of love.

—HENRY DRUMMOND

Everyone wants to be happy. Your ability to build and maintain long-term, loving, happy relationships with other people is central to your happiness, your health, and everything you accomplish in life.

Sometimes I begin a seminar by asking, "Who is the most important person in this room?"

People shout out different answers, "You!" or "The boss!" and finally some people say, "Me!"

At that point I say, "You're right! *You* are the most important person in this room. You are the most important person in your entire life. The entire world revolves around how you think and feel about it."

The Quality of Your Life

You are important. And how important and valuable you think you are largely determines the quality of your life. Virtually all of your problems in life—personally, professionally, and politically—stem from people who do not consider themselves to be particularly valuable, important, or significant.

Personal and social problems, personality defects, crime, antisocial behavior, and even international problems are all rooted in a feeling of not being important, not being good enough.

People who like themselves and consider themselves to be valuable and worthwhile people have high levels of self-esteem and self-respect. The more you like and respect yourself, the more you like and respect others, and the more they like and respect you right back.

How Much You like Yourself

It has been said that everything we do in life is either to gain self-esteem or to protect our self-esteem from being damaged. Your level of self-esteem, how important you feel you are, determines the quality of your inner and outer lives.

Most of your happiness and success will be determined by your relationships with other people, both at home and in the world around you. How well you get along with others largely determines the quality of your marriage and your parenting, your level of pay and promotion, and your success in life and your career.

The more positive you are as a person, the more people want to hire you, promote you, buy from you, socialize with you, date you, marry you, and be around you.

High-self-esteem parents raise high-self-esteem children. High-self-esteem bosses create high-self-esteem, high-performance workplaces. People with high self-esteem are the most liked and desirable people in your world.

Make Others Feel Important

The key to success in human relationships is simple: *Make others feel important.* Build their self-esteem at every opportunity.

Everything you do or say to make other people feel important raises their self-esteem and sense of personal value. When you make people feel important, they like and respect themselves more. They like and respect you more as well, and are open to being guided, directed, and influenced by you.

Daniel Goleman, author of *Emotional Intelligence*, was interviewed in *Fortune* magazine once and was asked, "What is the most important single quality of emotional intelligence?"

He replied, "Of all qualities, your level of *persuasiveness* is the very best measure of how fully integrated you have become." The height of your self-esteem largely determines your level of persuasiveness, and how much influence you have on others. How much you like yourself largely determines how important you make other people feel when they are around you.

You have heard the saying "I do not love you for who you are, but for how you make me feel about myself when I am with you." When people feel valuable and respected in your presence, you become a persuasive and influential person. Maya Angelou, the poet, wrote, "People will very soon forget what you said but they will never forget how you made them feel."

Build Self-Esteem in Others

There are five behaviors you can practice to build self-esteem in other people, make them feel important, and cause them to like you and want to help and cooperate with you. Each of these five behaviors begins with the letter *A*.

1. **Acceptance:** The root of self-esteem is *self-acceptance.* The amount that people accept themselves is largely determined by how completely they feel accepted by the people around them. The need for acceptance lies at the root of many behaviors, both personal and political. People cry out to be accepted just as they are, on their own terms. They often respond with anger and frustration when others reject them for any reason. For example, the critical point in the book and movie *Bridget Jones's Diary* is when she meets a man who likes her just the way she is.

   All of her friends are astonished! They cannot believe that there is actually a man out there who would like a woman just the way she is.

   When you like and accept people as they are, you appeal to one of the deepest emotions in human nature: the desire for unconditional acceptance by other people. And how do you express acceptance? Simple. You just smile.

   There's an old saying that it takes more muscles to frown than to smile. When you smile at another person, you simultaneously acknowledge her value, approve of her appearance, and express your enjoyment at being in her company. When you smile at another person, she feels more valuable and important, and her self-esteem goes up. Sometimes a smile can be so powerful that it changes a person's state of mind, attracts her irresistibly to another person, and often leads to people getting married and settling down happily for the rest of their lives.

The best news of all? Everything you do to raise the self-esteem of someone else raises your *own* self-esteem as well. In the Bible it says, "It is more blessed to give than to receive." In other words, what this means is that you get more personal pleasure and satisfaction out of giving of yourself and accepting others than they receive. When you go through your day doing and saying things that make people feel more valuable and important, you feel more valuable and important yourself.

Similarly, anything you do or say that hurts or reduces the self-esteem of another person also hurts and reduces your self-esteem. If you become negative or angry toward another person, you feel negative and angry toward yourself at the same time. The more kindness and warmth you express to another, the more kindness and warmth you have for yourself.

2. **Appreciation:** Each person has a deep, inner need to be appreciated for who he is and what he does. Whenever you express appreciation to another person for any reason at all, his self-esteem immediately goes up. He likes himself more, and as a result, he likes you even more because it is you who are generating this feeling in him.

For example, I had a friend in college who received a

valentine's gift from his girlfriend that made such an impact on him he couldn't help but tell everyone. I have never forgotten how she did it. She sat down and made a list of one hundred reasons why she loved him. Imagine getting a list from someone important to you telling you one hundred reasons why you are important to him or her. It may change your life forever.

And how do you express appreciation? Simple. You say thank you on every occasion. This phrase seems to exert a magical effect on other people. Whenever you thank and appreciate a person, she feels more valuable. She feels that what she is doing is better and of a higher quality. The more you thank people, the more likely they are to do higher-quality work. The more you thank people, the more motivated they are to do the same things that caused you to thank them in the first place.

Over the years, I have traveled in more than 120 countries. The first words I always learn when I go to a new country are *please* and *thank you*. You can get by anywhere in the world by saying please and thank you on every occasion. Doors will open for you, people will help you, and everyone will smooth your way.

In your family and in your work, continually smile, and say please and thank you on every occasion, even if there is no reason. Whenever I talk to someone in my business, I end the conversation with a thank-you. In a way, I am thanking people just for being alive. And people always respond positively and warmly when you express appreciation to them and for them.

EXERCISE: Give your significant other or some other important person in your life a list of ten things you appreciate about him or her.

3. **Admiration:** Abraham Lincoln said, "Everybody likes a compliment." Whenever you compliment another person for anything, his self-esteem goes up and his self-respect increases. He feels happy about himself, and happier about being in your presence.

The more *specifically* you admire something in the life, work, or personality of another person, the greater the impact it has on his feelings about himself.

People are very proud of the traits that they have developed over the course of their lives, sometimes with great effort and discipline. They are always flattered when somebody notices a particular trait that they have invested so much time and effort in developing. Examples: "You are very punctual." "You are highly disciplined." "You are a good listener."

You can compliment people on their surroundings: "This is a beautiful office," or "This is a lovely living room." People invest a lot of time and thought in their surroundings, and they are always flattered when you notice and compliment them.

You can compliment people on their personal possessions or clothing: "That is a great-looking briefcase." "That's a beautiful purse." "That suit looks good on you," or "That dress fits you perfectly." As long as your compliment is genuine, people will immediately feel happier and more important when they receive a compliment from almost anyone for almost any reason.

4. **Approval:** It is said that "children cry for it and grown men die for it."

One of the definitions of self-esteem is the degree to which a person feels himself to be praiseworthy. Praise satisfies one of the deepest cravings of human nature.

Whenever you praise a person for anything, large or small, you immediately raise her self-esteem and increase her sense of personal value and importance.

In business, approval and recognition go hand in hand. Whatever you approve of and recognize in another person, you will get more of. The more you approve of the behavior of a person in a particular area, the more she will repeat that behavior so she can get even more approval and recognition in the future. The use of continual approval is a wonderful way to build habitual behaviors in others, both adults and children, that are helpful both to them and to you.

When it comes to less desirable behaviors, if, instead of criticizing a person for poor performance, you simply ignore it, the poor performance will gradually stop. When you simultaneously give approval and recognition for an excellent job or performance, the person will be motivated to do more and more of the things for which she gets positive rewards, and fewer of those things for which she gets no comment at all.

The key to approval is to make it specific and immediate. Instead of saying to your child, "You're a great kid!" you can say, "You did an excellent job cleaning up your room this morning." Instead of saying to your secretary, "You're doing a wonderful job," you should say, "You typed out that report beautifully with no mistakes. You are really excellent at what you do!"

You will get more of whatever you approve. So approve *specifically*, and approve as soon after the act as possible for maximum impact. If a person does a great job at the beginning of the month and you don't mention it until the end of the month, it has very little motivational power. All the impact of the approval will have been drained away by time.

But when you praise a person immediately after he has done something positive or helpful, you dramatically reinforce the likelihood that he will repeat that behavior in the near future.

Furthermore, when you praise people in front of others, you multiply the impact of that praise on their self-esteem and their subsequent behavior. Ken Blanchard, in his book *The One Minute Manager*, recommends that you "catch people doing something right."

When you praise people in front of others and even brag to others about the superior performance of the individual who is standing there, he or she usually feels flattered, embarrassed, and motivated all at the same time.

When you praise a person in front of a group of people, you multiply the positive emotions that person will feel.

You dramatically increase the likelihood that he or she will eagerly repeat that behavior in the future. You simultaneously motivate the others who are applauding to want to engage in that behavior themselves so that they can receive public and private praise and approval.

APPRAISE IN PRIVATE

If you must give feedback to a person because of poor performance of some kind, always do it privately, out of sight and earshot of other people. This dramatically reduces the negative impact of a performance appraisal and makes it more likely that the individual will listen to what you are saying and do better next time.

EXERCISE: Choose three people whom you rely on and tell them something they are doing well. Be sincere and specific.

5. **Attention:** One of the most powerful ways of telling people that they are important and raising their self-esteem is called *listening.*

    Effective people are good listeners. Popular people are good listeners. Leaders are listeners. Instead of talking all the time, the most liked and respected people are absolutely excellent at listening closely to others.

Instead of talking, they ask questions. There seems to be a direct relationship between the number of questions you ask and how much people like and trust you. There's also a direct relationship between the number of questions you ask and the amount of time you can listen. And the more you listen to another person when he or she is speaking, the more that other person will like and trust you, and is open to being influenced by you.

FOUR KEYS TO EFFECTIVE LISTENING

There are four keys to effective listening:

1. **Listen attentively, without interruptions.** Lean forward and face the other person directly. Be an active listener: Nod, smile, and agree while the other person is speaking, and make no attempt whatsoever to interrupt or to comment on what she is saying.

   When a person is intently listened to by another, that person experiences measurable physiological changes. Her heart rate increases. Her galvanic skin response goes up. And best of all, her brain releases endorphins, nature's "happy drug," which gives the person speaking a feeling of importance, value, and self-esteem.

2. **Pause before replying.** Instead of jumping in with the first thing that comes to your mind, pause in silence after the person has finished expressing himself.

   Pausing has three advantages: First, you avoid the possibility of interrupting if the other person is just gathering his thoughts. Second, by pausing quietly, you tell the person that you are carefully considering what he has said because it is important to you. Listening tells the other person that his words are important and therefore *he* is important.

Third, when you pause before replying, and leave a silence in the conversation, you actually *hear* what the other person is saying at a deeper level. His words soak into your brain and you recognize nuances that you would have missed if you had immediately started speaking.

Remember, it is not what is said so much as what is *not* said, or what is said between the lines, that contains the deeper meaning of the message the other person is attempting to convey. By pausing after the other person has spoken, you become a dramatically better listener. You actually hear better.

3. **Question for clarification.** Never assume that you know what the person meant by what he or she said. If there is any question in your mind at all, after the person has finished speaking and you have allowed a certain period of silence, you can ask, "How do you mean?"

    One of the most important rules in relationships is: The person who asks questions tends to have control of the conversation. The person who asks the questions demonstrates a genuine interest in the other person. When you ask a sincere question or series of questions and listen intently to the answers, you guide the entire direction of the conversation. This builds greater trust between you and the other person. And the more you listen, the more the other person feels valuable and important. The more you listen, the higher is the self-esteem and self-respect of the person being listened to.

Perhaps the most important rule in conversation is: Listening builds trust. There is no faster way to build a warm and trusting relationship, in business or personal life, than to ask sincere questions and then listen closely to the answers, for as long as the other person wants to talk.

4. **Paraphrase what the other person has said.** Feed it back in your own words before you go on to speak yourself. Each person has a deep need to be understood by others. The way you clearly convey that you have understood both the words and the meaning of what the person has said is by rephrasing it in your own words and having him or her acknowledge that you have got the message.

Before you comment or respond, stop for a moment and say, "Let me make sure I understand what you are saying [or feeling]. From what you just said, I get the impression that this is how you think and feel . . ."

When the other person says, "Yes, that's it, that's what I'm trying to say," only then do you respond with your point of view.

PRACTICE PLAYING "FEEDBACK"

Feedback is an exercise that couples who argue a lot are taught to practice to improve their relationship. Here's how it works.

When the partners begin arguing, they agree that they will play feedback in this argument. One person then has an opportunity to express her thoughts, feelings, and reasons for her unhappiness or dissatisfaction. But before the second person can reply, he must feed it back to the original speaker in his own words. The first speaker must listen attentively, without interrupting, and—after clarifying any misconceptions—finally say, "Yes, that's my point. That's how I think [or feel] on this issue."

Only when the first person agrees and accepts the interpretation by the second person can he give his point of view on the situation. Then she has to feed that back to him to his satisfaction.

This simple exercise dramatically reduces the arguments or disagreements that take place in many relationships. This is because it is almost impossible to argue *slowly*. When a couple is forced to slow down and feed back to the other person exactly what the other person has just said, most of the heat goes out of the argument. It is replaced by a sincere desire on the part of both people to understand each other.

PRACTICE MAKES PERMANENT

You can practice the five A's of self-esteem building, of making people feel important, in every interaction with others, from the time you get up in the morning, throughout your day, and into the evening. Start with your family before you go to work.

You can practice acceptance by smiling at people and showing them that you genuinely care about them and like them. You can express appreciation by saying thank you on every occasion for both small and large actions. You can express admiration on a regular basis for the things that people have or the qualities that they demonstrate. You can express approval by praising people on every occasion for large and small accomplishments. And you can pay attention by listening closely to others when they want to speak.

Initially, the practice of these behaviors may require tremendous discipline on your part, especially if you have not been practicing them in the past. But as Goethe said, "Everything is hard before it's easy."

The more you deliberately practice raising the self-esteem of others and making them feel important, the more automatic and easy it will become, until it becomes a normal and natural part of your conversation. As you practice the five A's, your own self-esteem will go up as well. In no time at all, you will be getting along wonderfully with the important people in your life.

Marriage and Relationships

Marriage and intimate relationships are the most important, intense, and emotional relationships that you form in your life. Your ability to enter into a happy relationship with another person is a true measure of the quality of your personality. One of your great goals in life is to learn how to build and maintain a superior relationship with at least one other person.

Although every relationship is different, all of them have certain essential elements in common. When you can identify the most common problem areas and resolve them, you can dramatically improve the happiness of your relationship with that other person.

ELEMENTS IN COMMON

All relationships are based on certain key principles. When you can identify these principles and analyze them in terms of your own relationship, you can often find ways to dramatically increase your happiness and the happiness of the other person.

Even though you read a lot about the divorce rate in our

society, the fact is that about more than half of men and women marry one person and stay happily married to that person for the rest of their lives. Although there are a large number of divorces, they are usually concentrated among people who had difficult up-bringings and strained relationships with their parents. They did not see or witness two people in love and happily married as they were growing up, and as a result, they often find it difficult as adults to form a happy marriage themselves.

Many people who get married and divorced often get divorced two and three times, and even more. This dramatically inflates the divorce statistics. But in general, by practicing some of the principles of good relationships and removing some of the causes of bad ones, you can live happily for a long time with another person, perhaps for the rest of your life.

There are six major problems that lead to unhappiness, frustration, and even the breakdown of the relationship. Once you remove these obstacles, your relationship will be much smoother than before.

1. **Lack of commitment:** For a relationship to be successful, both parties must be totally committed to it. There must be a 100 percent, wholehearted decision to make this relationship succeed. In the absence of this total commitment, the relationship can start coming apart at the seams, especially under stress, which always occurs.

    One of the manifestations of a lack of commitment is shown in what is called the *go halfway* relationship. This occurs when one or both parties decide that they will go only halfway toward making the relationship work.

Many working couples marry and then carry on as if they are single people living together. They keep separate bank accounts. They divide the family expenses equally and keep careful notes on who has paid what amounts for things like rent, utilities, and telephone.

A lack of commitment in a relationship is often manifested by a prenuptial agreement, protecting each party in case of a divorce, which almost always follows. When people enter into a prenuptial agreement, they are anticipating the failure of the relationship and making provisions for what they will do when they go their separate ways. This falls into the category of the self-fulfilling prophecy, and is almost always realized.

Lack of commitment is based on the fear of failure, the fear of making a mistake by marrying the wrong person, and regretting it afterward. Because of this fear of failure, learned in early childhood, the adult often holds back and gives only as much of him- or herself as is necessary to keep the relationship going.

A lack of commitment leads to feelings of insecurity, especially on the part of the other person. It is said that in many relationships, there is someone who loves more, and someone who loves less.

The person who loves more is always willing to put more of him- or herself into the success of the marriage. The person who loves less continually withholds total commitment from the relationship, increasing the feelings of insecurity and inadequacy in the other person.

When a person is a victim of a lack of commitment on

the part of the other, which is manifested in continual criticism, he tends to feel that he is inferior, inadequate, and not worthy of being completely loved. This creates tension, stress, arguments, depression, and even physical and mental illnesses.

The solution for a lack of commitment is simple: Make a total commitment to the marriage from the first minute that you decide to get married. Put your whole heart into it. Hold nothing back. Combine all your resources as a single unit. Dedicate yourself to the success of this relationship above all else.

A WORD FROM CHRISTINA

Damon and I decided early on in our relationship that we were committed 110 percent to each other. As in every relationship, we have hit some speed bumps along the way, but we both know that, no matter what, we have committed to resolve whatever issue comes up. Neither of us ever doubts the other's total commitment. This creates tremendous security in our relationship. It provides lots of room for us to find ways to navigate our conflicts and to assure that we enjoy mutual satisfaction and happiness in our marriage.

Here are two important points:

1. If you cannot commit wholeheartedly to a marriage or a relationship, you should not enter into the relationship in the first place.

2. When you do make a total commitment to another person, you will often feel completely liberated. By giving up your freedom you will actually gain a tremendous sense of freedom. You can let yourself go completely by totally dedicating yourself to one person.

2. **Trying to change the other person or expecting him or her to change in some way:** There is a saying used by farmers: "Never try to teach a pig to fly, for two reasons. First of all, no matter how hard you work, the pig is never going to fly. Second of all, it just *irritates* the pig."

In emotional terms, trying to get someone else to change a fundamental behavior or characteristic is suggesting that the person is not good enough as she is. Instead of expressing unconditional acceptance of the other person, you are rejecting a fundamental part of her personality or behavior. When you try to change another person, you are attacking her sense of personal value and lowering her self-esteem. Because people cannot change, even if they want to, trying to change another makes her feel frustrated, and often trapped.

The antidote to trying to change another person is complete acceptance of the person with all of her qualities, positive or negative—to love her just the way she is.

The deepest need that human beings have is to be unconditionally accepted by the most important people in their lives, especially their partners.

A WORD FROM BRIAN

After my wife and I had met and fallen in love, we moved in together. One day, she sat me down and asked me to tell her all the things about her that I didn't like so that she could start working on herself to change them. She wanted me to be happy in our relationship.

After straining my mind for a while, I finally told her that I couldn't think of anything about her that I would change. I loved her completely, especially for her character and her personality. I was quite satisfied. There was nothing that I would want to change for any reason.

Because of her upbringing, and the criticism she had experienced in the past, she was very skeptical of my answer. She accused me of holding back. She said that I was not being sincere and honest with her.

For several weeks, she would bring up this subject again and again, and ask me to be honest with her and tell her what it was about her that I didn't like so that she could change it. I gave her the same answer every time. I couldn't think of anything about her that I didn't like.

Finally, one day, a light went off in her mind. It suddenly dawned on her that I was telling the truth. She was absolutely amazed. She had gotten the idea that she had certain qualities that were not acceptable. She had a false belief that she had to let go of, and she did. We have been happy ever since.

This is the way a happy marriage should be. Both parties should completely accept each other unconditionally, recognizing that no one is perfect, and neither asking nor expecting the other person to change.

3. **Jealousy:** This is one of the worst of the negative emotions. It can cause tremendous unhappiness in the person experiencing the jealousy, and in the person at whom it is directed.

The feeling that no one could ever really love the jealous person completely is the root cause of this negative emotion.

The propensity to experience jealousy comes from destructive criticism and lack of love in early childhood. The child grows up feeling that he is somehow inferior or inadequate. As an adult, he continually compares himself negatively to others.

When the jealous person enters into a romantic attachment or relationship, he is plagued by a tremendous sense of insecurity and the feeling that the other person will find that he has fundamental flaws.

The antidote to jealousy is high self-esteem. The more you like and respect yourself, the less concerned you are about the behaviors of the other person that would normally trigger feelings of jealousy. Your need is to realize and accept that you are a thoroughly good person, and that your value is inherent; it has nothing to do with the opinion of another person about you.

4. **Self-pity:** Self-pity is usually a habit that you learn from one of your parents. Throughout your childhood, one of your parents continually talks about how bad she was treated in life and how hard her life has been as an adult.

Alexander Pope wrote, "As the twig is bent, so is the tree inclined." The way your dominant parent, the parent you most identify with, thought, talked, and behaved when you were growing up has an inordinate impact on the way you think, talk, and behave as an adult. Self-pity is often caused by a lack of goals, a lack of meaning and purpose in your personal life. When you have no clear sense of direction, and you feel that you are merely reacting and responding to other people's demands, it is easy to start to feel sorry for yourself. You can start to see yourself as a victim of circumstances rather than a victor over circumstances.

The antidote to self-pity is simple: Get so busy working on your goals and doing things that are important to you that you don't have time to feel sorry for yourself. (We will show you how to do this in the next chapter.)

Take this as an example: Ellen grew up listening to her mother talk about all the things she wished she could do. Ellen would ask her when she was going to do them and her mother would always have a reason why she couldn't; she was too busy taking care of everyone else. Her mother's attitude of self-pity was very frustrating to her, and she believed her mother was making a choice. Ellen resolved at a young age that she would be different. As a result, she grew up committed to at least try to follow her dreams and pursue her passions. She refused to waste her life like her mother had. She did the opposite of what her mother had done.

A true sense of self-esteem comes from what is called *self-efficacy*, the degree to which you feel that you are competent at what you do. When you do something well and complete it, your sense of self-efficacy jumps, and so does your self-esteem. You see and feel yourself as a more important and valuable person.

The more you like yourself, the less you feel sorry for yourself. As you work on yourself and your goals, you soon reach the point where you feel terrific about yourself and all sense of self-pity disappears.

5. **Negative expectations:** This problem in marriage has its roots in early childhood, when you are the victim of the negative expectations of your parents. Whenever they criticized you and told you that you were not particularly good at something, you unconsciously began to expect to do poorly in that area.

When you get married, you often have a series of expectations of how the other person should behave, and how things should be in a marriage. If these expectations are not met, you feel frustrated and angry. You often lash out and demand that the other person change his behavior so that it is consistent with what you originally thought it was supposed to be.

The antidote to negative expectations is to always expect the best from your mate. Tell your partner that you think he is a wonderful person, and that he is competent, capable, and attractive. Since expectations will always be fulfilled, if you and your mate have high, positive expectations of each other, you will both strive to live up to those expectations in a positive way.

6. Incompatibility: This is perhaps the most common reason for failure in marriages and relationships. A marriage or relationship begins when two people are attracted to each other because they find each other compatible in some way—usually physically at the beginning, and then later, they find other areas that they have in common.

When people are in their twenties, they grow and change at the most rapid rate of adult life. Many people who get married in their early twenties find that by their late twenties, they have become completely different people. They are no longer compatible. They no longer have very many things in common, except perhaps their children, if they've had any together. Often this can lead to marital conflict and unhappiness, if not separation and divorce.

LAUGHING TOGETHER

One of the best indicators that incompatibility has set in is how little a couple laughs together anymore. The first thing that disappears when a relationship starts to sour is the laughter.

The second thing that goes is conversation. Soon, out of habit and inertia, people find themselves sharing the same house, watching television together, but having very little in the way of meaningful interactions or connections with each other.

The question you have to ask when you start to see signs of incompatibility in your relationship is: "Is this a fact or is it a problem?"

Of course, you should make every effort to find areas of commonality, and to reawaken the original attraction that brought you together. But if the relationship has gone cold and you have become different people with little in common, you often have to accept that this is a fact you cannot change, not a problem you can attempt to solve.

EXERCISE: People change together or they change and grow apart. Having common goals, values, and appreciation keeps you growing together. To determine how compatible you and your partner are, grab a piece of paper and a pen and write down your answers to the following questions: What do you and your partner have in common? What things do you enjoy doing together? What sort of things do you talk about? The longer the list, the better your compatibility is!

If incompatibility has set into your relationship, the practice of denial is very stressful. It can make you physically and mentally ill. It can lead to frustration, anger, arguing, and blowing up at each other for apparently no reason at all.

The key to dealing with incompatibility is to accept that if it has occurred, *no one is guilty*. Both parties have done the very best they can. If incompatibility occurs, it is something that just happens, like aging or the weather.

MAKING YOURSELF MISERABLE

Many people make themselves miserable for long periods of time by allowing themselves to become angry at the person who has fallen out of love, or who has changed so much that the partners have little in common to share. But the other person is not bad, evil, or guilty. He or she is just no longer compatible with you.

If incompatibility has set in, you should do everything you possibly can to save the relationship. Many times, going to a marriage counselor and talking about what brought you together originally can reignite the relationship. Going on a vacation with just the two of you for a few days can often rekindle the spark that brought you together in the first place. Taking a long trip in which you have many hours to talk can bring you back together again.

Incompatibility can set in if you both get so busy with your work or family life that you don't take the time to communicate on a regular basis. As a result, you start to become interested in different things and grow apart.

Whatever happens, listen to your heart. Make your decisions in your relationship solely based on what you feel is the right thing to do. If you are no longer compatible, accept it as a fact of life and deal with it in a mature fashion. Remember, it's not your fault. No one is to blame. No one is guilty. It just happens.

One more point on problems with marriages or relationships: Remember the *99-to-1 rule*. This says that people spend 99 percent of their time thinking about themselves and only 1 percent of their time thinking about everyone else in the world. For this reason, you should never stay in a relationship because you are concerned about what others might say or think about you if you broke it off. The fact is that no one is thinking about you at all.

Successful Relationships

There are six keys to successful relationships of all kinds:

1. **Compatibility:** You will always be happiest with someone who is similar to you in interests, tastes, and especially in values and attitudes.

   A good measure of compatibility is how you enjoy spending leisure time. People who are compatible enjoy the same leisure activities. And this is very important. No matter how good your sex life is, most of your life together will be spent in non-romantic activities, such as reading, movies, travel, vacation, and sports.

   A couple I knew, friends in high school, got married in their early twenties. They were both young, but he liked staying at home in the evenings, reading, watching television, and playing with their children. She liked going out to nightclubs, dancing, socializing, and behaving as if she was still single. This conflict over leisure activities eventually led to the collapse of the marriage.

   Another sign of compatibility is that you feel comfortable and relaxed with the other person's ideas and opinions. In areas such as politics, religion, and attitudes toward family and friends, you are both quite similar.

2. **Opposites attract:** You have heard this said many times, but it is true only in the area of temperament. In all other

areas, opposites cause conflict and lead to stress, disagreements, arguments, and unhappiness.

In the area of temperament, two people of opposite dispositions are usually most attracted to each other. If he is outgoing, she will be more introverted. If he is emotional and opinionated, she will be calm and rational. They will balance each other.

One of the ways to measure the compatibility in a relationship between two people is called the *conversation test*. It turns out that each person has a need to talk and a need to listen, in different proportions. Some people have a high need to talk and to talk all the time. Other people are comfortable speaking very little and listening a lot. This type of couple would be quite compatible.

A problem that arises very soon in a relationship is when both people like to talk a lot and are therefore frequently interrupting each other. There is continual competition over "airtime." Either one or both parties feel frustrated because they do not get to satisfy their need to talk.

The opposite can be equally bad: Neither is particularly talkative, creating long periods of uneasy silence between the two people. You sometimes see couples driving along or dining in restaurants, and neither is talking. These people are too similar in temperament and are therefore not meant for each other.

The true measure of compatibility in a relationship is that the temperaments are balanced, and both people get to talk all they want to talk and listen all they want to listen. In addition, there are comfortable silences in the relationship. The couple can sit or drive together quietly without either feeling uncomfortable or the need to speak all the time.

3. **Total commitment:** This is essential to happy relationships and perhaps the most important factor of all. It's well known that love is the total commitment to the development of the full potential of the other person.

You can tell when you love another person when his or her happiness is a central concern of yours, and the key to your own happiness as well. You are dedicated to making the other person happy most of the time.

4. **Genuinely liking (not just loving) each other:** This is an important ingredient for successful relationships and marriages. People are initially drawn together by the emotions of love and passion. But in the course of a relationship, they can have heated arguments and disagreements. Because of this, it is essential that two people not only love each other but also *like* each other. These are two separate issues.

You can measure the quality of your relationship by what is called the *best friend test.*

When you are in the right relationship with the right person, that person is your best friend. There is no one else in the world you would want to spend time with. There is no one in the world you would tell things to more freely and openly than your best friend.

Many people say, when they meet their ideal mate, "I finally found my best friend."

Sometimes people refer to this as having met their "soul mate" or the "love of my life." By definition, your best friend is someone who knows you very well and accepts you unconditionally for the person you are.

You can have many arguments and disagreements in a marriage, but as long as you continue to admire and respect your partner, your relationship can stay strong, year after year.

5. **Having similar attitudes and outlooks:** These people are the most compatible. You will always be most compatible with someone who is just about as happy and positive as you are. In fact, people with negative self-concepts are often attracted to each other and live together quite comfortably.

   Many people make the mistake of marrying someone who is unhappier than they are, with the firm belief that they will make the other person happy as well. But anyone who has ever gotten into a relationship with an unhappy person has discovered the awful truth: The positive person does not bolster the negative person and brighten up his or her mood and outlook. The negative person usually drags the positive person down. Soon incompatibility, unhappiness, and frustration set in and the relationship comes to an end.

6. **Communication:** This is the real key to happy relationships. The quality of your communication determines the quality of your life in every area, especially in marriage.

In a way, it is true that men are from Mars and women are from Venus, as the classic book title says. Men and women think, feel, and communicate differently from each other. It is essential for your happiness that you recognize the difference in communication styles and build them into your interactions with the other person.

According to MRI scans, when a man communicates, he uses only two centers of his brain. But when a woman communicates, she uses seven. Women have far more complex inner lives than men do. They think, question, evaluate, wonder, and dwell upon subjects, especially their relationships, far more than men do. If you ask a woman what she is thinking about or how she feels about something, she will always have a detailed answer.

Jerry Seinfeld said in a comedy skit that women are always wondering what men are thinking about, and the answer is simple: "Not much!"

Research shows that when a man and woman sit together watching television, 80 percent of the man's brain shuts down while the sound and images of the television program go past. The woman sitting next to him has fully 80 percent of her brain lit up, like a Christmas tree, while she watches the program and thinks of many other things at the same time.

In relationships, men tend to be more direct and women tend to be more indirect. To communicate more effectively, women often need to become more expressive and direct to get their point across.

For a man to communicate more effectively with a woman, he must listen patiently and attentively while she talks, without making any attempt to interrupt or add his opinions or points of view.

ATTENTION, AFFECTION, AND RESPECT

The primary needs that women have in relating to men are attention, affection, and respect. They need to be listened to and taken seriously. They need to know their partners are putting aside all other concerns and concentrating on what they are saying, thinking, and feeling.

Both men and women can improve the quality of their communications by practicing the four listening skills discussed earlier. They can listen attentively, without interrupting. They can pause before replying, to carefully consider what the other person has said. They can question for clarification, to be sure that they understand what the other person meant, and they can feed back what the other person has said in their own words to assure clarity of understanding.

Achieve Your Full Potential

You grow toward the realization of your full potential only when you are in a healthy, happy relationship with someone you love, respect, and admire, and someone who loves, respects, and admires you.

The building and maintaining of high-quality relationships is the key to health, happiness, and true joy in life.

You can become much better at building a high-quality

relationship by setting it as a goal and working on it all the time. In the final analysis, your own level of self-esteem, self-respect, and personal pride is the key factor in determining the quality of your relationships with others.

Most of your negative emotions, those destructive feelings that hold you back and undermine your happiness, are associated with your relationships with other people, past and present. As you become a more positive, optimistic person, your relationships improve in every area. As your relationships improve, and you feel loved and respected by the important people in your life, most of your negative feelings dissipate and disappear like cigarette smoke in the air.

✦ ✦ ✦

CHAPTER SEVEN

Get On with It!

There is one quality that one must possess to win, and that is definiteness of purpose, the knowledge of what one wants, and a burning desire to achieve it.

—NAPOLEON HILL

Now that you have released your brakes and removed your limitations, you are ready to make the rest of your life the best of your life.

You know that your life is what your thoughts make of it. You *do* become what you think about most of the time. Your thoughts and the way you interpret your past and present determine your feelings. Your feelings determine your actions and your results.

By taking complete control of your mind, the only thing over which you have complete control, you can change the entire direction of your life. Remember, you *choose* what thoughts to have more of and which thoughts to have less of.

Positive or Negative Thinking

The most positive, optimistic, happy people in every area think very differently than average people whose emotions go back and forth continually, sometimes positive, sometimes negative.

Many people are easily influenced by the most recent event that has occurred, or by the last person they spoke to. They change their minds and emotions quickly, and then change them again.

Most people have had difficult experiences growing up. They have had problems in adult life. If they are not careful, they can cling to these experiences, continually reviewing and rehearsing them, keeping them alive, sabotaging themselves year after year. This is not for you. You must choose to let go of these past experiences and move forward.

Fill Your Mind with What You Want to Be

The key to success, happiness, and complete fulfillment is to fill your mind with thoughts, words, images, and emotions consistent with the person you want to be and the life you want to live. To truly get on with your life and realize your full potential, you must become powerful, purposeful, and self-directed. That is what you will learn to do in this chapter.

The Seven Keys to Great Achievement

There are seven key parts of your life in which you must develop absolute clarity in order to unleash all your mental, physical, and emotional powers toward great achievement.

1. **Values:** The happiest and most effective people are very clear about their values—what they believe in and what they stand for. Unhappy, average people are unsure of their values, if they have any at all.

   Values clarification is one of the most important exercises you can do in your life. Begin by writing out a list of the three to five values or virtues that are most important to you. Then resolve to organize your life around these values, and stick to them without compromise.

   Many of the ancient philosophical greats, from Plato and Socrates to Aristotle, have identified certain virtues and values that seem to form the character of exceptional people. Among these are *integrity, courage, persistence, generosity, compassion, love,* and strong family relationships and *friendships.*

   There are dozens of values that you can use to form the foundation of your character. But those are some of the very best, and they are the values that most great men and women are known for.

   So how can you tell what a person's true beliefs and values are? It's pretty simple: Look at his actions and behaviors, especially what he does under pressure, when he is forced to choose.

   If you want to know the true character of a person, just watch how he behaves in the face of difficulties or when he is under stress. As the Stoic philosopher Epictetus taught, "Circumstances do not make the man; they merely reveal him to himself."

How do you develop a value or a virtue as a permanent part of your personality? The answer is simple: You practice that value whenever it is called for. By the *law of practice*, whatever you do repeatedly soon becomes a new habit, and stays with you permanently.

If you decide that patience is one of your most important values, then you resolve to practice patience in every situation in which it is called for. If you want to develop courage, you must practice courage whenever you feel afraid. If you want to develop the quality of integrity, then you resolve to speak and act honestly in every situation in which it is required. By practicing the values that you most admire, you can program them into your personality.

Your life is lived from the inside out, and your values form your inner core. When they are clear, strong, uncompromising, and positive, they give you a strong character and a pleasing personality. A person with clear values is more positive, has a firmer handshake, makes more direct eye contact, and even walks and moves with greater strength and purposefulness. This is your goal.

EXERCISE: Write down your top three to five values. Next to each, write a short description of how you behave when you practice that value. Why is this value important to you?

2. **Vision:** Once you are clear about your values, the virtues that you stand for, and the principles that you will not compromise, create your vision of your ideal future life and conditions as organized around your values. Idealize and visualize.

   To do this, project forward five years and imagine that your life is perfect in every way. What would you be doing? What would your life look like? What would be your situation in your work, family, and personal lives? And especially, how would your perfect life be different from today?

EXERCISE: Cut out a picture or pictures from a magazine illustrating your ideal life and self sometime in the future. Tape the picture up where you can see it every day, such as on the fridge or bathroom mirror. Continually imagine yourself living your ideal life.

We talked about idealization earlier as part of future orientation. The happiest and most successful people are very clear about where they want to be in the long term. The greater clarity you have about your future, and the more consistent it is with your values, the easier it is to make the necessary decisions each day that will eventually enable you to get to where you want to go.

3. **Mission:** What is your mission in life? What do you want to accomplish by applying your personality, intelligence,

ability, and skills to your world? What kind of a difference do you want to make in the lives of other people, especially your family?

One of the ways to determine your mission is to imagine writing your own obituary, to be read at your funeral and published in the newspaper. What would you want it to say about you, and about what you accomplished in life? What would you want your obituary to say about the effect you had on the lives of other people, and how you will be remembered?

The greater clarity you have about how you want to be thought about after your departure, the more likely it is that you will do and be the kind of person who leaves that kind of legacy behind.

EXERCISE: Write your own obituary. Describe the kind of person you became in your life and the qualities you would like to be remembered for. Think about how you would have to live your life for your obituary to be true.

4. **Purpose:** You need absolute clarity about your purpose on this earth. Every person is born with a special reason for being here. What is yours?

Why do you get up in the morning? Why do you do the job you do? Why are you in that relationship, or raising that family? What is your real purpose? Where do you want to end up?

A review of more than five hundred biographies and autobiographies of noteworthy men and women found that the one common quality among them was that, from an early age, these people had a "sense of destiny." They absolutely believed that they had been put on this earth to do something special with their lives, something that would help to improve the lives of other people in some way. Whether it was Albert Schweitzer, Mother Teresa, Winston Churchill, Ronald Reagan, or Pope John Paul IV, each was convinced that his or her special talents and gifts belonged to all of mankind.

In order to be purposeful in your achievements and your life, you must have a purpose. In order to be focused and channeled, you must have a direction. Keep asking yourself, "If I had no limitations on what I could be, have, or do, what would be my vision, mission, and purpose in life?"

5. **Goals:** You need clear goals and plans for every area of your life. It is said that success is goals and all else is commentary.

To achieve your full potential, you must have clear, written goals that you are working toward achieving each day. Without goals, you can just go around in circles, working for years and making very little progress.

Thomas Carlyle wrote, "A man without goals is like a ship without a rudder. He makes no progress on even the smoothest seas. But a man with goals is like a sailor with a rudder, a map and a compass who makes progress on even the roughest seas, and sails to his destination."

7 STEPS TO SET AND ACHIEVE YOUR GOALS

Here is a proven seven-step goal-achieving process that you can use for the rest of your life:

STEP 1: Decide exactly what you want and write it down clearly and specifically on a piece of paper. People with clear written goals earn, on average, ten times as much as people without written goals.

STEP 2: Set a deadline on your goals. Write down a specific date by which you intend to achieve each goal. If it is a major goal, such as financial independence, you could set your deadline ten or twenty years down the road. You then set sub-deadlines for a series of interim goals that you will have to accomplish each month or each year to achieve your major goal.

The greater your clarity with regard to your goals and the greater the emotion with which you energize them, the faster you accomplish them. The more positive you are about achieving your goals, the faster you activate all your mental faculties. You begin moving ahead at a rate that you may have never experienced before.

STEP 3: Identify the difficulties you will have to deal with, the problems you will have to solve, and the obstacles you will have to overcome to achieve your goals. Write them down. Review this list and identify the single biggest ob-

stacle, either within yourself or within your world, and resolve to work on that major obstacle before anything else.
Note: The operative word here is *major*. There are no significant obstacles or difficulties standing between you and
your goals or if they are minor annoyances you're facing,
you're not reaching high enough or being ambitious enough
with each goal and it is merely an activity. For example,
getting to work through morning traffic is not a goal. Increasing your income, building a successful business, achieving
financial independence, and losing weight are all goals because they require effort, determination, and persistence,
and there is never any guarantee you will achieve them. The
point is to tackle a challenge that will vault you forward in
your progress toward achieving what you desire in life.

STEP 4: Identify the additional knowledge and skills that you
will have to acquire or hire in order to achieve your goals.

Remember, whatever got you to where you are today is
not enough to get you any farther. To get ahead, you must
master new knowledge, skills, and abilities. Whatever they
are, identify them clearly, write them down, and then make
a plan for their attainment.

STEP 5: Identify the people, groups, and organizations
whose help and cooperation you will require to achieve your
goals. You need the help of lots of people to accomplish big
goals. No one does it by him- or herself.

Remember, when you think of the people whose assis-
tance you'll require, always ask yourself, "How will they

benefit?" People do things for their own reasons, not for yours. Resolve in advance to be a "go-giver" rather than a go-getter. Look for ways to help people achieve their goals in the process of helping you to achieve yours. A mutually beneficial situation is far more appealing for everyone and builds community and connection.

STEP 6: Make a plan. Take all the elements that you have identified in the first five steps of this process and list them on a piece of paper. A plan is a list of activities organized in two ways. First, it is organized by *sequence*: What do you have to do first? Second? Third? What do you have to do before you do something else? Create a checklist.

Second, a plan is a list organized by *priority*. What is more important and what is less important? Apply the well-known 80/20 rule to your list. What 20 percent of your activities can potentially contribute 80 percent of the results you want to achieve? Discipline yourself to start on these activities first, before you do anything else.

STEP 7: This is the most important step of all. Once you have decided upon your goals and organized your list of activities by sequence and priority, *take action immediately*. Do something as soon as you can. The faster you start working to achieve each goal, the quicker you will complete it; the sooner you will focus all your resources toward the attainment of that goal.

(For a complete goal-setting program, at no charge, go to www.briantracy.com.)

Resolve to do something *every day* that moves you in the direction of your most important goal. Every morning when you get up, think about at least one step you can take that day that will move you closer to the attainment of that goal. Resolve to do something every day, seven days a week, 365 days a year, without fail.

When you do something every day, you trigger the magic power of the *momentum principle*. This principle says that it may take ten units of energy to get started on a new goal, but once you start moving, it takes only one unit of energy to keep moving forward. When you force yourself to launch toward your goal, you break the bonds of inertia that hold most people in place, and you begin to unleash all of your powers.

6. **Priorities:** You need clear priorities to determine what is important and valuable to you, and what is not.

You cannot manage time itself; you can only manage yourself and how you spend yours. Time management is life management. Time management is the ability to choose the sequence of events. It is the ability to choose what you do first, what you do second, and what you do not at all. And you are always free to choose. This is the key to success in life.

You will always be overwhelmed with too much to do and too little time. No matter how clever you are in organizing your time and your work, you will never get caught up. Throughout your life, you will continually have to set clear priorities on the use of your time, based on the value of that activity compared with anything else you could do at that moment. To accomplish anything of value, you must be able to set priorities and stick to them.

7. **Actions:** Once you are clear about your values, vision, mission, purpose, goals, and priorities, you must have the willpower and discipline to launch yourself into continual action in the direction of your dreams.

Throughout this book, we have explained the central role of self-esteem in success, happiness, and good relationships. The core driver of self-esteem is *self-efficacy*. This is defined as how effective you feel you are at doing what you are doing, and how competent you feel to achieve your goals.

The more you like yourself, the better you do almost everything in your life. And the better you do the most important things in your life, the more you like yourself. Self-esteem and self-efficacy reinforce each other.

Performance-Based Self-Esteem

This brings us to what is called *performance-based self-esteem*. It seems that you truly like and respect yourself only when you know, deep down inside, that you are good at what you do, and that you are capable of setting and achieving the goals that are important to you.

People who have never set and achieved a major goal always experience feelings of inadequacy and insecurity. They doubt themselves and their abilities. They are never sure of themselves and are plagued by fears of failure and rejection. As a result, they play it safe, and settle for less in life than is truly possible for them.

But people who have set and achieved one or more big goals

are filled with confidence and enthusiasm. The very thought of a new challenge raises their self-esteem, increases their courage and confidence, and propels them forward toward the achievement of even bigger goals in the future.

Remember a Big Success

You can probably relate to this idea. Think about something you worked hard to achieve and how you felt when you had accomplished the task. You felt more capable, more confident, and more in control of your life.

The achievement of success is not the most important thing. What is most important is the person you have to become, the character and qualities that you have to develop in order to achieve that success in the first place.

To achieve something that you have never achieved before, you must become someone you have never been before. You must do things you have never done before, over and over again, until you actually become a new person.

You actually shape and sculpt your personality and develop your character to a higher level as the result of your clarity about your goals and your persistence in achieving them.

Pushing to the Front

The most productive and effective people tend to have an intense *excellence orientation*. They are determined to be very good at what they do. They think about excellence and high achievement all the time. They are never satisfied with their current level of performance. They are always raising the bar on themselves.

In my twenties, I was unemployed and hungry to succeed at

something—anything. I finally found a job in straight commission sales, knocking on doors throughout the day and into the evenings. One day, the top salesman in my company said to me, "Did you know that you have to be in the top 20 percent of people in this business if you want to make the big money?"

When I heard that, I was initially crestfallen. I had never been good at anything in my life. I had dropped out of high school and worked at laboring jobs for several years. I was struggling as a door-to-door salesman at the time, and now I was told that I would have to be among the best if I wanted to succeed in this field, or any other field.

A REVELATION

Then I learned something that changed my life: Everyone in the top 20 percent of their field started off in the bottom 20 percent. Everyone who is doing well today, in any field, was once doing poorly. Everyone who is at the front of the line of life started at the back of the line.

Everyone in the top 20 percent in your field today was at one time not in your field, and did not even know that it existed. But no one is better than you and no one is smarter than you. If someone is *doing* better than you, it is simply because he or she has learned the critical skills necessary in that field and practiced them more often than you have. And what others—sometimes hundreds of thousands of others—have done, you can do as well.

ALL SKILLS ARE LEARNABLE

This realization changed my life. Then I got another shocker. I discovered that all business skills are learnable. All technical skills are learnable. All career skills are learnable. As with reading, writing, and arithmetic, no one starts off with these skills; everyone has to learn them over time.

All business skills are learnable. All sales skills are learnable. All money-making skills are learnable, as well. And anything that hundreds of thousands, even millions of other people have learned, you can learn as well. No one is better than you and no one is smarter than you.

This revelation changed my life. From that moment onward I became a dedicated student of personal and professional development. I read every book and article I could find that would help me to improve my performance. I listened to audio programs while walking around and in my car. I attended every seminar and workshop I could find. I later took thousands of hours of university courses to upgrade my knowledge and skills so that I could achieve my goals faster and more predictably.

The Magic of Personal Development

Personal development changed my life. It made me a completely different person. Over the years, I have worked with hundreds of thousands of people in eighty countries who have said the same thing. Almost all of them started off from humble beginnings. They had achieved everything they had achieved through hard work and commitment to developing themselves and their abilities. And what other people all over the world have done, you can do as well.

Another wonderful thing about personal development on your journey to excellence is that each time you learn something new that can help you, your self-esteem goes up. You feel happier and more in control of your life. You feel more powerful and have greater self-respect. It is not just the ultimate goal of becoming excellent in your field that contains the payoff. It is every step along the way.

Be the Best at What You Do

Just as goal achieving changes your character, becoming excellent at what you do changes your character. The only way that you can truly enjoy high levels of sustained self-esteem and self-confidence is when you know, deep in your heart, that you are very good at what you have chosen to do. And once you have that, no one can ever take it away from you.

Abraham Lincoln said, "The only security that a person can ever have is the ability to do a job uncommonly well."

Here is a question for you: What one skill, if you were absolutely excellent at it, would help you the most to move ahead in your career?

YOUR WEAKEST SKILL

It seems that your *weakest* important skill sets the height of your success, achievement, and income in any field. Bringing up your level of performance in your weakest skill area can do more to propel you forward than any other action you can take. Many of my students have doubled and tripled their incomes in just a few months by identifying their weakest skill and then committing themselves to mastering that skill in every way possible.

SET IT AS A GOAL

Once you have identified that one skill that could help you more than any other, apply the goal-setting process to developing that skill. Write it down as a positive affirmation: "I am absolutely excellent at . . ."

Write it down and set a deadline. Determine the obstacles you will have to overcome, the people whose help you will require, and the actions you will have to take each day. Make a list; organize it by sequence and priority. Take action on your new goal, and then do something every day until you are excellent at that skill.

Become Intensely Results Oriented

In addition to goal orientation and excellence orientation, the most successful people in every field practice intense results orientation. They think about results most of the time. They think about the most important things that they can do each day and each hour. They then discipline themselves to work on their top tasks most of the time.

In every field, people who work on the top 20 percent of their tasks (i.e., the tasks that have the biggest positive impact on their success) accomplish five to ten times as much as the average person, even though others may have the same level of knowledge, education, and skill.

In your work life, results are everything. They are the only thing that counts for success and advancement. They are the critical determinants of how much you are paid and how quickly you are promoted. Nothing can replace the need to get results in a steady, predictable, and consistent way. All top people focus on results most of the time.

Increase Your Productivity

To achieve more and better results, here are some key questions you can ask yourself every day:

1. **Why am I on the payroll?** What have I been hired to accomplish? Why do they pay me money at my job? What specific results am I expected to contribute to my company?
2. **What are my highest value-added tasks?** Of all the things that I do, which ones are more valuable than anything else in achieving the results that are most important to my company?
3. **What are my key result areas?** What are the five to seven tasks I do that make up my job? Where am I stronger? Where am I weaker? In what areas could I improve my knowledge or skills? Where do I need to work harder to master my key tasks?
4. **What can I—and only I—do that, if it's done well, will make a real difference to my company and my life?** This is something that only you can do. If you don't, no one else will do it for you. But if you do it, and you do it well, it can make a big difference in your work or in your personal life. What is it?
5. **What is the most valuable use of my time right now?** Helping you determine the most valuable use of your time at every minute is the final aim of all time-management exercises.

Focus on Your Contribution

The focus on results, on making a maximum contribution, is closely connected to your self-esteem and self-confidence. The more you feel that you are making a real contribution in your work and in your life, the more you like and respect yourself, and the happier you are. The more you contribute, the higher is your self-esteem. The more you contribute, the more you are esteemed and respected by the people around you. The more you contribute, the better results you get, and the more you feel in complete control of your life and your future.

Seven Keys to a Positive Personality

Mental fitness is like physical fitness; you develop high levels of self-esteem and a positive mental attitude with training and practice. Here are the seven keys to becoming a completely positive person:

1. **Positive self-talk:** Speak to yourself positively; control your inner dialogue. Use affirmations, statements phrased in the positive, present, and personal tense: "I like myself!" "I can do it!" "I feel terrific!" "I am responsible!"

   Most of your emotions are determined by the way you talk to yourself throughout your day. The sad fact is that if you do not deliberately and consciously talk to yourself in a positive and constructive way, by default, you will think about things that make you unhappy or cause you worry and anxiety.

   Your mind is like a garden: Either weeds or flowers will grow. But if you do not deliberately plant flowers, and tend them carefully, the weeds—the negative thoughts—will grow without any encouragement at all.

2. **Positive visualization:** The ability to visualize and see your goals as already realized is perhaps the most powerful ability that you have.

   Create a clear, exciting picture of your goal and your ideal life, and replay this picture in your mind over and over. All improvement in your life begins with an improvement in your mental pictures. As you see yourself on the inside, you will be on the outside.

3. **Positive people:** Your choice of the people with whom you live, work, and associate will have more of an impact on your emotions and your success than any other factor. Decide today to associate with winners, with positive people, with people who are happy and optimistic, and who are going somewhere in their lives.

   Avoid negative people at all costs. Negative people are the primary source of most of life's unhappiness. Resolve that from today onward, you are not going to have stressful or negative people in your life.

4. **Positive mental food:** Just as your body is healthy to the degree to which you eat healthy, nutritious foods, your mind is healthy to the degree to which you feed it with "mental protein" rather than "mental candy."

   You should read books, magazines, and articles that are educational, inspirational, or motivational. Read material that is uplifting and that makes you feel happier and more confident about yourself and your world.

   Listen to positive, instructive audio programs in your car

and on your smartphone. Feed your mind continually with positive messages that help you to think and act better and make you more capable and competent in your field.

Watch positive programs on YouTube, as well as TED Talks. Take online instruction on the subjects most important to you, and read other uplifting material that makes you feel good about yourself and your life.

5. **Positive training and development:** Almost everyone in our society starts off with limited resources, sometimes with no money at all. Virtually all fortunes begin with the sale of personal services of some kind. Most people who are at the top today were once at the bottom, and sometimes they fell to the bottom several times.

The miracle of lifelong learning and personal improvement is what takes you from rags to riches, from poverty to affluence, and from underachievement to success and financial independence. When you dedicate yourself to learning and growing, and becoming better and better in your thoughts, abilities, and actions, you take complete control of your life and dramatically increase the speed at which you move upward and onward to greater heights.

6. **Positive health habits:** Take excellent care of your physical health. Resolve today that you are going to live to be eighty, ninety, or a hundred years old and still be dancing in the evenings.

Eat excellent, healthy, nutritious foods, and eat them sparingly and in proper balance. An excellent diet will have an immediate positive effect on your thoughts and feelings.

Resolve to get regular exercise, at least two hundred minutes of motion per week, walking, running, swimming, bicycling, or working out on equipment at the gym. When you exercise on a regular basis, you feel happier and healthier and experience lower levels of stress and fatigue than a person who sits on the couch and watches television all evening.

Especially, get ample rest and relaxation. You need to recharge your batteries regularly, especially when you are going through periods of stress or difficulty. Vince Lombardi once said, "Fatigue doth make cowards of us all."

One of the factors that predisposes us to negative emotions of all kinds is poor health habits, fatigue, lack of exercise, and nonstop work. Don't let these happen to you.

7. **Positive expectations:** This is one of the most powerful techniques you can use to become a positive person, and to ensure positive outcomes and results in your life.

Your expectations become your own self-fulfilling prophecies. Whatever you expect, with confidence, seems to come into your life. Since you can control your expectations, you should always expect the best. Expect to be successful in advance. Expect to be popular when you meet new people. Expect to achieve great goals and create a wonderful life for yourself. When you constantly expect good things to happen, you will seldom be disappointed.

✦ ✦ ✦

Seven Truths About You

To be what we are, and to become what we are
capable of becoming, is the only end of life.

—ROBERT LOUIS STEVENSON

No matter who you are today, or what you have done or not done in the past, there are seven essential truths about who you are as a person, deep down inside:

1. **You are a thoroughly good and excellent person.** You are valuable and worthwhile beyond measure. No one is better than you and no one is smarter than you. In your heart of hearts, you are a fine human being. You are as good as or better than anyone you will ever meet.

2. **You are important, in many, many ways.** Of course, you are important to yourself. Your entire world revolves around you. You are the most important person in your personal universe. You give meaning to everything you

see or hear. Nothing in your world has any significance except for that which you attribute to it personally.

You are also important to your parents. Your birth was a significant moment in their lives and still affects them today. As you grew up, almost everything you did was important and significant to them.

You are important to your own family, to your mate, your spouse, your children, and the other members of your social circle. Some of the things you do or say have an enormous impact on them.

In your work, you are important to your company, your customers, your coworkers, and your community. The things you do or don't do can have a tremendous effect on the lives of others.

How important you believe you are largely determines the quality of your life. Happy, successful people feel important and valuable. Because they feel this way, they act this way, and it becomes true for them.

Unhappy people feel devalued and unimportant. They feel frustrated and unworthy. As a result, they lash out at the world and engage in behaviors that hurt themselves and others.

3. **You have unlimited potential.** You have the ability to create your life and your world as you desire. You could not use your entire potential if you lived a hundred lifetimes.

No matter what you have accomplished so far, it is merely a hint of what is truly possible for you. And the more of your potential you develop, the more you can develop in the future.

4. **You create your world in every respect** by the way you think and the depth of your convictions. Your beliefs create your realities. And every belief you have about yourself you have learned, starting in infancy. The amazing discovery is that most of the negative beliefs that interfere with your happiness and success are not based in fact or reality at all. They are not true.

5. **You are always free to choose.** You control the content of your thoughts and the direction of your life. You control your inner life completely. You can decide to think happy, fulfilling, uplifting thoughts, which lead to positive actions and results. Or you can, by default, end up choosing negative, self-limiting thoughts that trip you up and hold you back.

   Your mind is like a garden; either flowers or weeds will grow. But if you do not deliberately cultivate flowers, weeds will grow automatically, without any effort on your part. This simple analogy explains most unhappiness in life. People are not planting enough flowers in the form of positive, happy, uplifting thoughts.

6. **You were put on this earth with a great destiny.** You are meant to do something wonderful with your life. You have a unique combination of talents, abilities, ideas, insights, and experiences that make you different from anyone who has ever lived. You were designed for success and engineered for greatness. Your acceptance or nonacceptance of this truth largely determines your level of ambition and the direction of your life.

7. **There are no limits to what you can do, be, or have** except for those you place on your own thinking and your

own imagination. The biggest enemies you will ever have are self-limiting beliefs, beliefs that are not based in fact, but that you have accepted through the years until you no longer question them.

Remember this rule: It doesn't matter where you're coming from; all that really matters is where you're going.

Make a decision, right now, that you are going to unlock your full potential and become the extraordinary person who lies deep within you. You are going to accomplish the extraordinary things that you were put in this world to do.

Summary

You are a thoroughly good person. You are designed for success and engineered for greatness. You have within you more talent and ability than you could use in one hundred lifetimes. There is virtually nothing that you cannot accomplish if you want it long enough and hard enough, and are willing to work for it.

When you learn to release your mental brakes, forgive everyone who has ever hurt you in any way, and dedicate yourself to becoming an excellent person in your relationships with others and in your work, you take full control of your destiny. You maximize all of your abilities and put yourself on the high road of health, happiness, loving relationships, maximum achievement, and complete fulfillment.

There are no limits!

Photo by Michael Campbell

Photo by Josh Monnesson

BRIAN TRACY is chairman and CEO of Brian Tracy International, a company specializing in the training and development of individuals and organizations. He has studied, researched, written, and spoken for thirty years in the fields of economics, history, business, philosophy, and psychology and is the top-selling author of numerous books, which have been translated into dozens of languages.

CHRISTINA STEIN, Ph.D., is a speaker, author, and psychotherapist who runs a private practice in Santa Monica, California, focusing on work-life balance and male and female empowerment. She works with individuals and couples and conducts workshops to help attendees align their priorities and goals with their skills and passions. She holds a master's degree in clinical psychology from Antioch University and a Ph.D. from the Institute for Advanced Study of Human Sexuality.

Get Smart!

How to Think and Act Like the Most Successful and Highest-Paid People in Every Field

Brian Tracy

Bestselling author of *Eat That Frog!*

tp
tarcherperigee

VICTORY!

Applying the Proven Principles of
Military Strategy to Achieve Greater
Success in Your Business & Personal Life

BRIAN TRACY

Bestselling author of *Eat That Frog!*

tarcherperigee

ALSO FROM BRIAN TRACY

MASTER YOUR TIME MASTER YOUR LIFE

The Breakthrough System to Get More Results, Faster, in Every Area of Your Life

BRIAN TRACY

Bestselling author of *Eat That Frog!*

tarcherperigee